INTRODUCTION

There are many women in history whose lives were exceptional, interesting, and exotic. However, few of them took over, and forced history to see them for what they accomplished on their own by their strength of character and purpose. Men, who for centuries were the historians, downplayed their accomplishments or referred to them as "difficult, aggressive, self-obsessed, and sexually repressed, possibly physically cold." What could be the basis for these descriptions? Could it be male vanity and masculine jealousy?

Hopefully, this book will present these women with all of their faults, fears, and vulnerabilities as well as their courage and strengths.

I0170882

Author's Note:

The biographical material at the end of each chapter was designed for future reading about these wonderful "wicked" women. It does not include all of the information collected by the author. The book is not an academic project, so there are no footnotes, although most of the historians are quoted directly from their books. This was done to make further studies about the wonderful "wicked" women from sources easily obtainable and to make the book more readable. The original Latin sources were translated by the author and checked with other translations to secure accuracy.

Queen Elizabeth II's biographers claim that "indirectly" she is a descendant of King Arthur through her grandmother, the daughter of the 14th Earl of Strathmore. And the Picts in the north of England and the Iceni in the south disappeared into the milieu of people who make up Greater Britain. Somewhere in Italy are the great, great, great, etc. grandchildren of Zenobia, and lost in the Middle East are the descendants of Theodora. Hopefully, they inherited the great qualities of their predecessors.

TABLE OF CONTENTS

My thanks to the following people who helped me locate the wonderful "wicked" women and present them to you:

Carolyn Thorne, librarian and researcher, Technical Services Center, Dallas County Community College District.

Beverly Holmes, former library director, El Centro Community College, Dallas, Texas.

Mary Cecil Carington-Smith.

Bette Moscarello, typist and coordinator.

Hallie Garner, book preparation.

To my grandparents for their different perspectives on life:

Anglo-Irish—a good fight,

Jewish—education, education, education

Scottish—a love of the oceans and seas of the world,

Shawnee—storytelling and a profound respect for the
environment.

And, always, for Melody, the artist and the child.

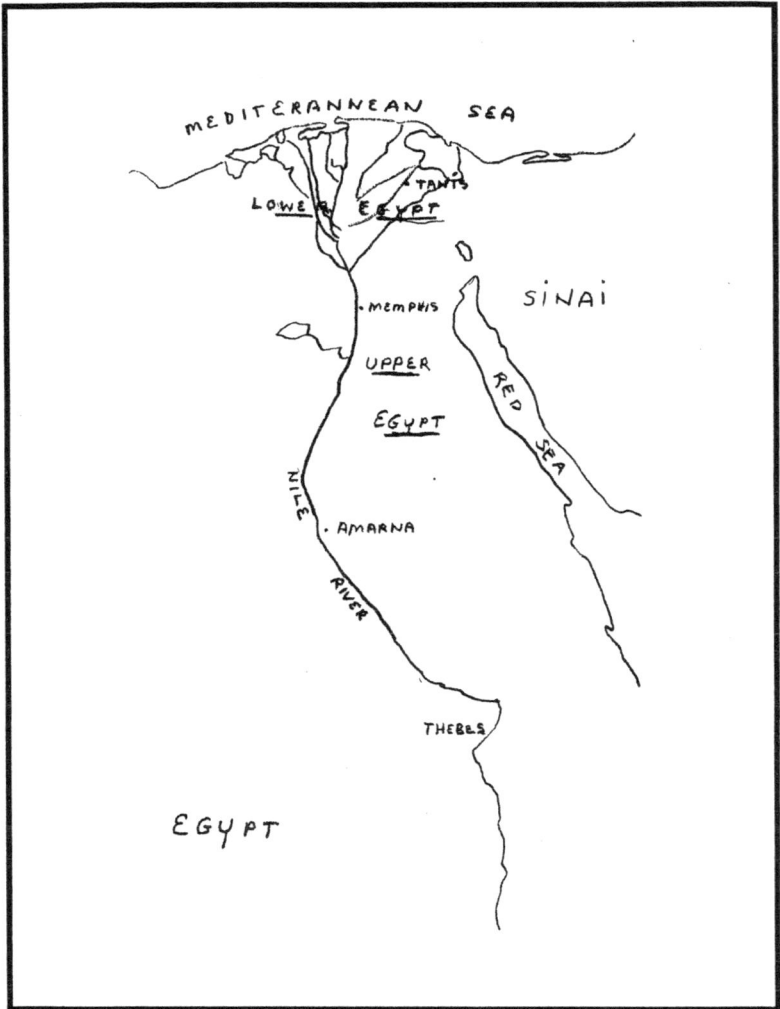

HATSHEPSUT

God's Wife and Mistress of the Two Lands. "The first great woman in history."

James Henry Breasted

Twilight is the best time to visit Hatshepsut's funerary temple at Deir el Bahri, when the Egyptian sun is descending behind the Valley of the Kings and the soft purple shadows stretch to the ascending temple ramps. The complex is framed by cliffs in deeper blue. The weathered white columns extend across the front of the temple on three different levels. The entire complex appears so simple, harmonious, and beautiful; it looks serene there in the dusk.

Across the centuries, especially at twilight, Deir el Bahri stands as a labor of love for the woman who was a pharaoh, Hatshepsut.

Early Eighteen Dynasty Dates (?)

Ahmose	B.C. 1575 - 1550
Amenhotep I	B.C. 1550 - 1528
Thutmose I	B.C. 1528 - 1510
Thutmose II	B.C. 1510 - 1490
Hatshepsut as regent and king	B.C. 1490 - 1468
Thutmose III	B.C. 1490 - 1436

These dates are those of Manetho, an Egyptian priest who wrote in the third century, B.C., fifteen hundred years after the reign of Hatshepsut. There are few sources to contradict his scramble of pharaohs and kings. However, because of Dr. Kate Spence, Egyptologist and former architect at the University of Cambridge writing in *Nature*, November 2000, this may change. Using modern astronomical calculations to check the movement of the North Pole to date the Great Pyramid of Khufu, Dr. Spence may force historians to re-date the time line of each pharaoh.

There is confusion and disagreement among historians as to Hatshepsut's familial relationship and her accomplishments in Egyptian history. At one time, her name was erased from the king list.

She was the daughter of Thutmose I of the Eighteenth Dynasty of Egypt who made herself male and divine. She "arranged" a biography in which the god Amun "descended" upon her mother, Ahmose, "in a flood of perfume and light." Amun then announced that Ahmose would give birth of a daughter "in whom all valor and strength of the god would be made manifest on earth."

Her name was Hatshepsut.

This story was important to Hatshepsut because it gave her a justifiable position in the pantheon of the kings of Egypt. After all, pharaohs were gods on earth. How to record a female king? When was this divine birth proclaimed? Was it before she made herself king* or during her regency when she ruled for Thutmose III, her stepson and nephew? In order to maintain the purity of dynastic succession in Egypt, kings could marry their daughters and sisters could marry their brothers. This proved to be somewhat successful for a time. It is possible that Hatshepsut could have married her father, brother, or stepbrother.

Did Hatshepsut's mother go along with this tale of her birth and assist in its dissemination? Both women understood court intrigue and

---

* It was not until the last years of the Eighteenth Dynasty that *pharaoh* was first used as the title of the king. Barbara Mertz, in *Temples, Tombs and Hieroglyphics* writes "Pharaoh comes from two Egyptian words meaning 'great house,' referring to the palace." All titles of kingship were masculine. What was a scribe to do with Hatshepsut?

survival. This may have been the story agreed upon because Thutmose II, Hatshepsut's half-brother, and her husband, was considered to be "weak-willed" and "physically delicate," dominated by his wife and mother. But he surprised them. As Donald Redford writes in his *History and Chronology of the Eighteenth Dynasty of Egypt*, Thutmose II appointed as his successor the son of a "lowly concubine in the temple of Amun, a mere child," to be Thutmose III. Who would guide him in his duties as pharaoh? Certainly not the lowly concubine. More important to Hatshepsut and Ahmose, was the status of this child in the Egyptian hierarchy. The prevailing story was that Hatshepsut was the only surviving daughter of Thutmose I and his wife Ahmose. In the family, Ahmose had the most credentials because she was a direct descendant of the Theban princes who had freed Egypt, driving the Hyksos invaders from the desert out of Egypt and restoring it to the Egyptian princes. She passed along those credentials to Hatshepsut, now the young dowager queen of Egypt, who was also called Great Royal Wife and Daughter of the King. Hatshepsut claimed that *she* was chosen by her father to rule Egypt, not the lowly born concubine and a little boy. So when Thutmose II died in 1504 B.C., she moved quickly to take over, first as regent, then as king. She claimed all of the titles as Lord of the Two Lands. The only title of Egyptian kingship she did not claim was "Mighty Bull" for obvious reasons.

A statue of Hatshepsut in the British Museum in London gives a hint of a slim, rather small, almost fragile woman with a gentle face and a pointed chin. Her eyes slant slightly, and they were probably black. She is sometimes shown in a man's kilt and a royal collar, wearing the ceremonial beard of office (nothing else), with the crowns of Upper and Lower Egypt firmly atop her female head. Some historians have called her "a beautiful woman, gifted not only with every female charm, but with extraordinary intellect and a powerful personality as well."

And always at her side, was Senenmut, her architect and probably her lover. (For there is no evidence that he was not). Deir el Babri, her temple, is obviously a labor of love. "I have done this according to the design of my heart," was an inscription found hidden inside an inner room of the temple.

As a young man, Senenmut had served in the temple of Amun at Karnak. He probably was from humble beginnings, but he bragged that he was "the greatest of the great" and "the real favorite of the king." He was also the steward to Hatshepsut's daughter, Nefrure, and tutor of Thutmose III. In the Field Museum, Chicago, a statue of Senenmut shows him as a rather substantial person with big ears holding Nefrure.

Special consideration was given to the temple of Amun by Hatshepsut, either because of the influence of Senenmut and/or because the priests of the temple assisted her to power. Perhaps they helped to bring about her downfall as well by later supporting Thutmose III. As Pharaoh, he gave large grants of treasure and slaves to the temple of Amun at Karnak. Or it could have been the military that saw the way to power by training Thutmose III until he attained his majority.

Most historians believe Hatshepsut came to an "unnatural end." There were men who probably disapproved of a woman's involvement in politics anyway. There were merely four female pharaohs out of hundreds of pharaohs who ruled dynastic Egypt. Only Gay Robbins in *Women in Ancient Egypt* and P. H. Newby in *Warrior Pharaoh's,* suggest that her death might have been of natural causes. However, in her regna year 22, about 1468 B.C., Hatshepsut disappeared, as did Senenmut and other officials of her reign. Her daughter had died before her mother's

7

disappearance.

It was then that Thutmose III became pharaoh and immediately marched to Megiddo to defeat Syria. He ruled for more than three decades and made himself master of the eastern Mediterranean. She died or was killed; he lived and became Egypt's "greatest military ruler."

However, before Egypt became a military state under Thutmose III, Hatshepsut's rule of more than twenty years brought peace and prosperity to Egypt by reopening gold mines, trade routes and completing a building program employing masses of workers. The prosperity of her reign provided the money for the armies of Thutmose III.

When she began her reign, she must have acted within the law or she could not have consolidated her position so quickly. First, she became regent and surrounded herself with able administrators. Not only did she appoint Senenmut; but also Nehesi, a Nubian and organizer of the voyage to Punt; Habusoneb, vizier and high priest of Amun, a combination of the temporal, spiritual, and politically astute; and an old military man, Amos Pen Nekhbet who had fought for six kings of Egypt.

Why appoint the leading general as a special advisor if she had no military ambitions? Most historians writing about Hatshepsut deny that she ever participated in a military campaign or had anything to do with military affairs. However, the evidence is fragmentary. Donald B. Redford, quoting information found in a 1957 translation of a Habachi text, denies this is true, and calls this "a lopsided view of Hatshepsut's reign." He writes that there is historicity for at least four military campaigns during her twenty-two-year reign. He lists a campaign against Nubia led by the queen; military operations in Palestine and Syria; capture of Gaza led by her stepson Thutmose III; and further campaigns against Nubia. Although she recorded no wars at Deir el Bahri, a Nubian is shown leading

8

captives to the queen. "Her arrow is among the northerners," translates James Breasted.

Does this mean that she participated in seizing the Retenue/Habiru by force and in collecting booty from the battlefield? Is it possible that Thutmose III, when he became pharaoh, destroyed the records of her conquests so there could be no comparisons made? He has been accused of destroying and mutilating her statues, and attempting to eliminate her memory; why not destroy records as well? Or is this the woman whose reign is described by J. Wilson and *the Burden of Egypt* as "peaceful, conservative and isolationist."

Breasted quotes her as writing, "My southern boundary is as far a Punt. . . . ; My eastern boundary is as far as the marshes of Asia. . . . ; My western boundary is as far as the mountains of Manu. . . . ; my fame is among the Sand dwellers." Breasted also writes that warfare was impossible for Hatshepsut, so her "achievements were in the arts and enterprises for peace." But was warfare impossible for her? Perhaps she made use of Thutmose III before he succeeded her, while he was a young man of about twenty in military training, practicing to become pharaoh. She could have gone into battle with him, riding her chariot, carrying a javelin. Most historians concede that in her years as pharaoh, there was no lack of food, full employment, trade with the eastern Mediterranean, and generally peace within Egypt.

However, there must have been some quiet doubt among the people as to her role of pharaoh. In the cliffs behind Deir el Bahri, John Romer, in his documentary *Valley of the Kings*, shows us a cave in which workmen gathered in a "drinking club," as he calls it. The workers and stonemasons had left behind jars of fermented beer for archaeologists to find. They also left behind on the walls, several pornographic depictions of a woman in the pharaoh's wig bending over while she is being sodomized by a male figure. Romer calls it a "political cartoon." It may have been merely the depiction of a disgruntled employee, a frustrated artist, or possibly evidence of underlying tensions in Egyptian society about Hatshepsut's role as pharaoh. It is in jarring contrast to the beauty of the temple complex below the cave.

In addition to Deir el Bahri, one of her two obelisks at Karnak remains a symbol of majesty. The four-sided spire, originally covered with electrum, (a combination of silver and gold) stood almost one hundred feet high, the largest quarried in Egypt. Senenmut had the obelisk completed in seven months. It was inscribed with cartouches, which are oval signatures of Hatshepsut. These were later covered over or rubbed out and replaced with names of other Thutmoses, to obliterate her memory, or in the cases of Rameses II, to take credit himself for the work of Senenmut. Hatshepsut also ordered the temples of her predecessors to be repaired; this pleased the gods, she believed.

With the help of Nehesi, she planned the first trading mission to Punt, called the land of the god. At the time, no one knew the location of Punt. Was it in Arabia? Ethiopia? Who were these people? Hatshepsut ordered artists to accompany the seven ships of the fleet to make sketches for reproduction at Deir el Bahri and scribes to give her details of this voyage.

The story of the expedition is told on the south side of her temple. The Punts are shown as being tall and fair with aquiline features. The men wore long, narrowed beards. The king and his sons are slim, but his wife is enormous, seated on a small donkey, and his daughter seems to favor the mother. The homes in Punt seem to be built on stilts on the banks of a tidal river, probably near the coast. The people were friendly and interested in trade. John A. Wilson writes that they were amazed by the sailors and asked, "How did you reach here, this country unknown to men?"

The seven ships of Egypt returned home with "exotic" and "fabulous things." Each ship carried an incense tree, "carefully packed, with earth around the roots." These myrrh trees were planted in the terrace areas at her temple, along with palms and other "sacred trees." Ebony, ivory, gold, cinnamon, baboons, monkeys, panther skins went on display. This was a high point of Hatshepsut's reign.

But always in the background was the young Thutmose III for whom she had first acted as regent and then took over his throne. What had he been doing during her twenty-two-year reign? Senenmut had initially tutored him, and then he entered military training. He was young when he fought in Syria, with or without Hatshepsut. This experience was necessary for a future pharaoh, because Egyptian society wanted protection of its borders and the trade routes to the north. After the Hyksos invasion and their forcible removal from Egyptian soil, people demanded that the country be protected from foreign invaders, so a strong military was deemed a necessity. Thutmose III obviously learned his lessons well, because Breasted describes him as "the world's first empire builder" who designed "exquisite vases at his leisure; a lynx-eyed administrator" of whom it was said, "there was nothing of which he was ignorant."

How did Hatshepsut control so strong an individual? Why didn't she just kill him? It was done often enough in the royal house as wives and concubines fought to place their children in line for the throne. Perhaps it was because her only child had died and there was no heir. If she had married, her child would have had a better claim to the throne than

Thutmose III. But why share power with a husband when she had it all? Maybe murder was not within her psyche. Margaret Murray called her "a strong-willed, noble-hearted woman."

Several historians, including Hans Goedicke and John Bimson have suggested that Hatshepsut could even be the Egyptian princess who rescued the infant Moses from the bulrushes and brought him up in the palace. She certainly had the power to do this. Could Hatshepsut and Thutmose III have been pharaohs during the Exodus?

Thutmose III, always technically pharaoh or co-pharaoh, would have been sent north to Lower Egypt for military training, because that is where Asiatics fled in times of drought and fortresses protected "the way of the sea," the only direct northern route through Sinai. Were these "garrison cities," where Israelites were "forced to make bricks," in biblical Goshen? Could Moses, who had some military training, have been in the court with Hatshepsut and Thutmose III and witnessed what was happening to his people, or to the "mixed, classless assortment" of those making bricks?

It would have been impossible to escape the area because of the troops and because of "the Wall of the Ruler." When archaeologists could find no wall, it was assumed that flooding of the Nile each year would have destroyed or buried it in mud. Then, with NASA technology, a canal was discovered. Filled with crocodiles, the canal would have been a formidable "wall."

As Moses and Thutmose III, at the subsidiary court in the north, grew older, they could have confronted each other in Goshen. Goedicke remarks on Hatshepsut's displeasure at the Asiatics there and having "to restore good order to them" several generations after Ahmose I had expelled them from Egypt. This would have been the job of Thutmose III.

Two momentous happenings also could have occurred at this time:

the eruption of the Thera volcano on Santorium, or the biblical plagues. Either of which could have caused the rapid downfall of Hatshepsut. Egyptian scribes never wrote about bad things that happened, so there is no record of either of these events, although the disastrous effects of Thera were felt across the eastern end of the Mediterranean Sea. The pharaohs, as gods, were supposed to protect Egypt, not bring its destruction. The threat could have brought her removal from the king lists and from the throne. Within weeks of her disappearance, Thutmose III was campaigning in Canaan. How could the Israelites have possibly left the wilderness while Thutmose III controlled the trade routes. Hatshepsut may have been blamed for these remarkable events and for bringing a curse upon Egypt by usurping the throne, successful as her reign may have been.

How, when and why did it all end for her "on the tenth day of her regnum year, twenty-two." Mertz theorizes that a Syrian uprising might have taken place, combined with a shift in power among the military or the religious. Thutmose III was in his prime, trained militarily. He stepped in and took over as rightful heir and never looked back. What happened to Hatshepsut? Sterndorf and Seale write that about 1482 B.C. Hatshepsut came "to an unnatural end." Thutmose III then "wreaked with full fury his vengeance on the departed ones." Did he assist in their "departure?" Breasted accuses him of sheathing her obelisk at Karnak and of covering her name. Then, "he commanded his people to take hammers and smash to pieces over a hundred stone statues of the queen." He had her name cut out and obliterated. She was not listed among the pharaohs of Egypt; her memory was wiped out.

Thutmose III went further and covered the name of her architects Senenmut and Thutiy. Even objects in Senenmut's tomb were mutilated, and an order given "that the tomb of the queen's chief steward be dealt with." It was. The sarcophagus was found by archaeologists in pieces. There was neither trace of his mummy nor that of Hatshepsut. The final indignity, writes Julian Huxley, "is that Thutmose III obliterated her name from many monuments and substituted his own." Mertz calls it "one petty act in a career generally free from malice or hate." Did he need to destroy her as a political necessity or to establish his legitimacy?

There is still another theory that a romantic might consider, since the mummies of Hatshepsut and Senenmut have never been found; they ran off together, south, possibly to Punt, into history, into the mysterious future, hand in hand. They just disappeared leaving it all to Thutmose III. Why would he pursue them? Senenmut had tutored him well, and Hatshepsut had left him with a prosperous country. Historians describe him as "strategist, statesman, and administrator."

As the years passed, and the memory of Hatshepsut faded, did the mighty, victorious pharaoh ever visit the temple at Deir el Bahri? In its quiet, darkened halls, did Thutmose III feel the divine presence of Hatshepsut? There in the lavender twilight not Thutmose III nor time have erased the magnificent temple that stands to the memory of Hatshepsut.

SELECTED BIBLIOGRAPHY

Robbins, Gay. "The Enigma of Hatshepsut" *Archaeology Odyssey*. Biblical Archaeology Society. Washington, D.C. Winter, 1999, pp. 30-41.

Breasted, James Henry. *A History of Egypt From Earliest Times to the Persian Conquest.* New York: Charles Scribner's Sons, 1937. A monumental work. First Egyptologist to work with hieroglyphics.

_____*Ancient Records of Egypt, Vol. II.* New York: Russell and Russell, Inc., 1962. Contains the hieroglyphics with the translation.

_____*Ancient Times, Vol. I* : Boston, Mass.: Ginn and Company, 1963.

Durant, Will. "Our Oriental Heritage," in *The Story of Civilization Vol. I.*, New York: Simon and Schuster, 1954.

Gardener, Sir Alan. *Egypt of the Pharaohs.* Oxford University Press, 1961.

Murray, Margaret. "Queen Hatshepsut" in *Kings and Queens of Ancient Egypt.* London: Hodder and Stoughton Ltd., 1924.

Huxley, Julian. *From an Antique Land.* London: Max Parrish, 1955.

Mertz, Barbara. *Temples, Tombs and Hieroglyphs.* New York: Dell Publishing Company Inc., 1964. The first historian who writes about Hatshepsut as a king *and* as a woman.

Newby, P. H. *Warrior Pharaohs.* London and Boston: Faber and Faber, 1980.

Redford, Donald B. *History and Chronology of the Eighteenth Dynasty of Egypt: Seven Studies.* Toronto: University of Toronto Press, 1967. Redford presents a different view of Hatshepsut as a warrior queen.

Robins, Gay. *Women in Ancient Egypt.* Cambridge, Mass.: Harvard University Press, 1996.

Romer, John. *Valley of the Kings.* Company Ltd., 1981. Producer: Paul Watson: Lionheart Television, BBC in America, 1981. A documentary filmed in the cliffs above Deir el Bahri that shows possible dissatisfaction during the reign of Hatshepsut.

Spencer, Kate. "Ancient Egyptian Chronology and the Astronomical Orientation of the Pyramids." *Nature,* Vol. 408, No. 6810, pp. 320-325.

Steindorf, George and Searle, Keith C. *When Egypt Ruled the East.* Chicago: University of Chicago Press, 1942, (reprint 1957).

Wilson, Ian. *Exodus: The True Story.* San Francisco: Harper and Row, 1985.

Wilson, John A. *The Burden of Egypt.* Chicago: University of Chicago Press, 1967.

Hatshepsut's Obelisk amid the ruins of Karnak.

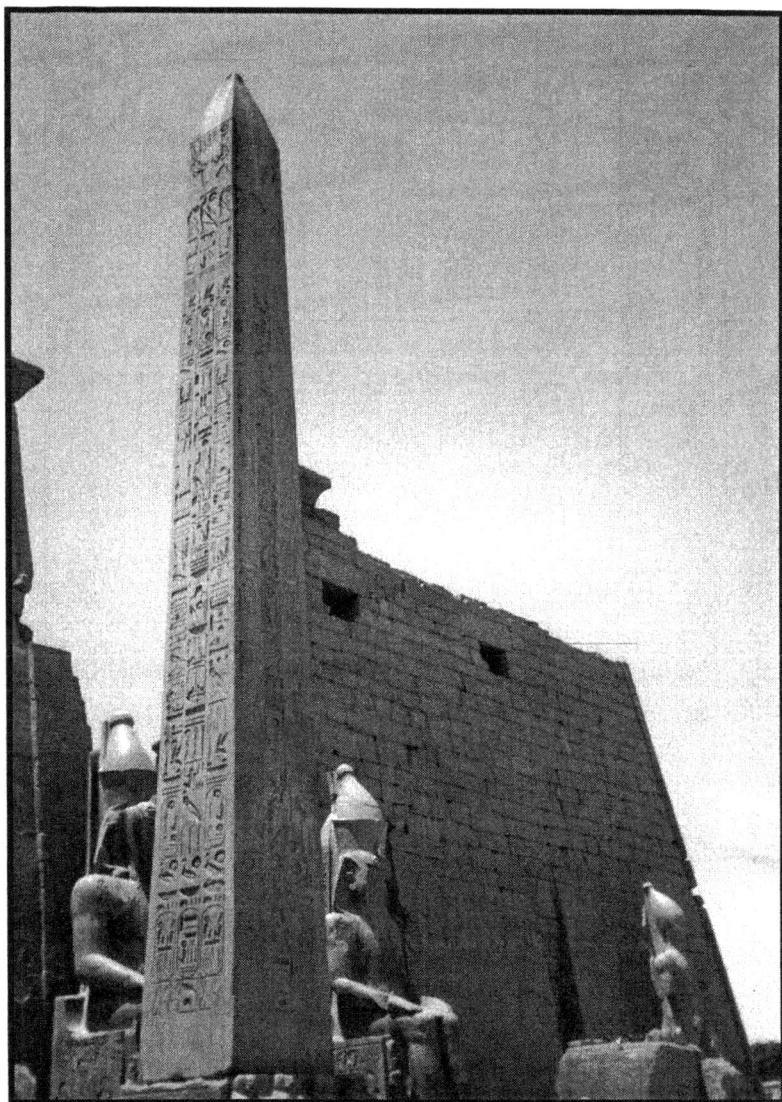

Hatshepsut's Obelisk at Karnak.

BOUDICCA/BOADICEA

"I am avenging my lost freedom, my scoured body, and the outraged chastity of my daughters."

Cornelius Tacitus, quoting Boudicca

In the center of London, a town she once destroyed, there is a fifty-foot high Victorian statue of Boudicca. Within sight of Big Ben and the House of Commons, it commands the Thames embankment. With sword in hand and arms upraised, Boudicca urges her warhorses onward. The Roman legions may have ultimately defeated her in battle, but to the British her name in Latin translates to Victorius and as far as history is concerned. she was.

Boudicca in London. *Picture courtesy of Edward S. Gregory, III.*

In A.D. 43, Emperor Claudius made Britain a Roman province. The native people, called *Britanni* by Julius Caesar, were too busy fighting each other to unite and force the Romans back across the Channel.

Why the Romans bothered to extend the empire beyond the continent is a matter of speculation. The island was close to Gaul, so supplying troops against barbarians who needed "Roman culture" would be relatively easy. There were rumors of pearl fisheries, but it may have been that the army and the generals, who often became emperors, saw it as one more conquest at the edge of the western world.

The original inhabitants of Britain after the ice age were Celtic-speaking tribes later pushed into Wales in the southwest and into Strathclyde in the north. The tribes were annexed first and subdued later by the Romans. Edward Gibbon in his *History of the Decline and Fall of the Roman Empire* paints a vivid picture of the subjugation: "A war of about forty years, undertaken by the most stupid, maintained by the most dissolute, and terminated by the most timid of all the emperors."

He describes the defeated tribes of Britons as possessing "valor without conduct, and the love of freedom without the spirit of union."

As for Boudicca, he writes that despair could not avert the slavery of her country when "the throne of Rome was disgraced by the most vicious of mankind." The warrior queen tried to save her small portion of Britain occupied by the Iceni from Roman pillage, rape and slavery. She failed, but ironically, it was a Roman historian, Cornelius Tacitus, who wrote of her courage and of the 2000 legionnaires, eight cohorts and a thousand cavalry sent by the emperor to put down her revolt. The Iceni were crushed, after which Rome developed a "milder policy."

Tacitus was a Roman senator and consul who wrote his *Annals* fifty years after the rebellion. He had access to the imperial archives, which contained the military reports from Britain. Tacitus was rediscovered during the Renaissance, and Boudicca became a heroine after more than thirteen centuries. Her story was preserved by a Roman whose father-in-law, Agricola, became governor of Britain. Tacitus wrote that after the rebellion was put down, and after the death of Boudicca, Agricola then brought "civilization to this rude, scattered, and warlike people." He doesn't write too much about the official inquiry or of Polyclitus, who headed the commission to investigate the causes of the revolt. But he does blame Boudicca for "this ruin brought upon Rome by a woman."

Before the rebellion, the territory of the Iceni was a relatively prosperous area. Tacitus described the people as having "horses, expensive gear, and finely wrought gold jewels." The king of the Iceni was Prasutagus, husband of Boudicca and the father of two daughters. When the Romans occupied southern Britain, the tribe had submitted peacefully, possibly because the merchants had been trading with the Empire and did not fear land confiscation. Prasutagus, Boudicca, and tribal elders were probably requested to be at Camulodunum when Emperor Claudius had a great ceremony to mark the unconditional surrender of "eleven conquered British kings," which for the first time, "reduced the barbarians beyond the sea under the power of the Roman people."

The king retained "token" independence, but paid tribute and accepted monetary assistance or "loans" from Roman bankers, at high interest rates in order to become "Romanized" and to build a new house in "the Roman tradition."

Meanwhile, the Romans had set up a large military zone, a capital of the province of Britain at Camulodunum and a prosperous trading post that was London. The Roman army spread out from these centers, building forts and roads. Inside their vast area of influence, some of which was confiscated Iceni land, it was forbidden to carry arms, including the great iron sword of the Iceni, a mark of an aristocrat.

One group of the Iceni rebelled and was swiftly subdued. Prasutagus evidently did not participate in the rebellion because he retained his crown and the military did not move against him. The Romans, however, were not finished with the rebellious area. They set up a permanent colony at Colchester, near Camulodunum, for retired army veterans, giving them confiscated tribal lands. Here was a reserve of experienced soldiers who could fight for Rome and protect the land they had taken without giving compensation to the Iceni. They ran their new estates with British slaves. Colchester prospered and Romans in Britain had a good life.

Prasutagus must have known that his independence as a client king was precarious, so he took measures by which he hoped to protect his family and its inheritance: he made Emperor Nero his co-heir with his two daughters, believing this was his only option. It might have worked, but it did not. When Prasutagus died in A.D. 60, "after a life of long and renowned prosperity," Roman agents immediately arrived and plundered his household. Tacitus writes that Boudicca was whipped and her daughters raped. Roman veterans confiscated the remainder of Iceni lands.

Under Roman Imperial Law, the personal fortune of a "client King" became Imperial property at his death. Catus Decianus, aent of Nero, may even have operated with his approval when Prasutagus died and the special relationship ended. This is the reason the king had named Nero and his daughters as co-heirs. At the time of death, an inventory of lands, livestock, and jewelry had to be made. A collector of accounts would receive a percentage for doing the inventory. Collectors were usually old legionnaires.

When they appeared at the Iceni palace and demanded entry, they treated Boudicca as a barbarian. She resisted, of course, which was considered to be an act of rebellion. So the Romans moved in against a defiant queen, lashing Boudicca and raping her daughters.

Adding to the grievances of the tribes was a recall of all British loans by Roman merchants who were overextended and wanted their money. Back in Rome, moneylenders like the Emperor's tutor, Lucius Seneca, pressured their counterparts in Britain to collect money while they could. Seneca may have been a distinguished philosopher, but he also knew how to make money and he did so while he was an early advisor to an unstable Nero. When he fell from the emperor's favor, Nero advised him to take poison and end his life. He complied.

The rumblings of revolt among the Britons did not seem to affect the Romans who were confident in their military might and affluence. London had no fortifications or legions in residence. It was a growing center of commerce and banking. It was also the headquarters of procurator Catus Decianus, Nero's agent and tax collector. Tacitus wrote, "His rapacity caused the problem." Decianus also had the responsibility of maintaining the temple/cult of Claudius in Colchester, and the tribes were taxed for its upkeep. The procurator left for Gaul before the Iceni had an opportunity to revenge themselves upon him.

The governor of all Britain was Caius Suetonius Paulinus. He had gone west to attack Druid strongholds and end their influence on the tribes. He also had a project to advance the Roman Empire to the Irish Sea. In A.D. 61, he crossed the Menai Straits where Collingwood and

24

Myres wrote that he met "a strange and awe-inspiring assembly." There, before his troops were groups of warrior women bearing lighted torches, Druids in prayer in front of fires the Romans believed to be human sacrifices. "The Romans came ashore and killed them all."

In the middle of the massacre, Suetonius received word that the client kingdom of the Iceni was in revolt. He could not return his legions to the mainland before the first major attack by Boudicca on Colchester. Direct Druidic influence on the Iceni is not known, but Boudicca must have had information about the absence of Suetonius and what he planned to do to the Druids at Anglesey, because it was then that she decided to wipe out Colchester. She led the Iceni, Trinovantes, and other tribes who "secretly plotted together to become free again."

First, isolated Romans on Iceni land were burned out and killed. Then, Boudicca marched on to Colchester to destroy the temple of the "divine Claudius." After a two-day siege in which men, women, and children crowded into the temple, it was taken. Tacitus calls what happened "instant vengeance," because of the butchery that took place.

When the Ninth Roman legion, stationed in Cambridgeshire, heard of the disaster at Colchester, its impulsive commander Quintus Petillius Cerealis raced south hoping to catch Boudicca. But she waited and planned an ambush of the legion when it entered a forest northwest of Colchester. Her forces sprang from the forest and wiped out the infantry. Part of the cavalry escaped to warn London and Suetonius. When Suetonius arrived from Anglesey, he realized that he could not save London; it had no defenses. But he hoped to save Britain for Rome. He evacuated the town and left those who would not leave to their fate. He consolidated his troops and refugees into the military zone.

Along the way to London, the Iceni and Trinovantes stopped to loot and kill, taking back what was theirs. If they had quickly reorganized, they could have reached London before Suetonius and ambushed him there. But Suetonius was an experienced military commander who was leading disciplined troops. They were trained to move quickly and on command. The Britons, as described by Graham Webster, were "amateurs vs. professionals," without organization, discipline, or equipment. They fought naked, almost with joy. For them it was "blood sport."

Suetonius sacrificed London when he saw its lack of defenses. Those who did not leave were warned that the Romans could not save them. Suetonius then planned where he would meet Boudicca. Where would he have the advantage?

For the first time in its history, London burned. It had been a sprawling shanty-town of warehouses and merchants. Cassius Dio in his *Roman History* wrote that Boudicca's army took no prisoners. "They could not wait to cut throats, hang, burn and crucify." It was total destruction. Tacitus added to the account that "all those left behind were butchered . . . nor did they consider the money they could get for selling slaves, it was the gibbet, fire, and the cross." Boudicca looted Verulanium and St. Albans, too. Britons who had supported Rome barely had time to move to Basham Harbor and escape. It was the aim of the tribes to eliminate all Romans from Britain.

The final battle took place in A.D. 61. Boudicca decided to risk a pitched battle with the legion. Perhaps she hoped that another defeat would force the Romans to go home. Although Tacitus describes the last battle and gives a description of the battle, he does not give a precise location. It may have been on or near the military road, Watling Street that led to the Roman base, which could send reinforcements and supplies. With a "wide plain before him," and the woods behind him, Suetonius

26

deployed his legionnaires in the center with cavalry on the flanks. Boudicca's Britons outnumbered the Romans as much as 10 to 1. Women and children always accompanied the warriors to the battlefield to encourage them with screams and taunts to the enemy. But Graham Webster gave the edge to the Romans because they were well equipped and well disciplined. Their officers could move the troops to new positions rapidly and "control the course of action." They could "engage a horde and defeat it with fewer troops," while the Britons were committed "to charge and fight it out."

For both sides it was a defining moment. The Romans could lose the province of Britain and their lives. The Iceni and the other tribes could lose their homeland, their independence, and their lives.

Both Boudicca and Suetonius spoke to their troops. Tacitus writes that Suetonius told his men to

Ignore the racket made by these savages. There are more women than men in their ranks. They are not even properly equipped. . . . Knock them down with your shields and finish them off with your swords.

Boudicca must have made quite an impression on the assembled troops. The Greek historian Cassius Dio described her as being "huge of frame, terrifying of aspect," and "with a harsh voice." "A great mass of bright red hair fell to her knees. She wore a great twisted golden necklace and a tunic of many colors, over which was a thick mantel, fastened with a brooch." Dio continued that she was "possessed of greater intelligence than often belongs to women."

She was said to have grasped a spear as she spoke to the tribes:

But now it is not from a woman descended from noble ancestry, but as one of the people that I am avenging lost freedom, my scoured

27

body, the outraged chastity of my daughters . . . you will see in this battle, you must conquer or die. This is a woman's resolve; as for men, they may live and be slaves.

She reminded them that they had to ransom themselves every year with their taxes. "How much better is poverty with no master than wealth with slavery."

Where did these two historians get these speeches? Could they have made them up, hoping that they would be able to address troops like this if ever they were in command?

Boudicca's forces moved up to the Roman line and met a volley of javelins thrown into their crowded ranks. Too packed together to make use of their heavy iron swords, the Britons took a second javelin attack. Meanwhile, the Roman cavalry moved out and around them, pushing them into the semi-circle of carts filled with their families. Hemmed in, there they were slaughtered. Tacitus said at least 80,000 Britons died, while the Romans lost 400. Both figures may be exaggerated.

The battle had lasted most of the day as the legions charged again and again in their wedge-shaped formations. After it was obvious the Romans had won, surrounded by bodies of men, women and children, they remained in the field, pursuing any of the tribes who had escaped the battlefield. Suetonius had sent for reinforcements from Gaul. Even Titus, son of Vespasian and future Emperor, who had been fighting in Judea, arrived to help wipe out all resistance. The Romans ravaged the countryside, killing animals and destroying crops, so that "famine was a curse upon the land." Thousands died. Iceni territory in Norfolk was so punished by the victorious Romans that it lagged behind the rest of Roman Britain for 400 years. Not until a new governor, Petronius Turpilianus arrived that the military action ended the revenge for

Colchester and London.

A new generation grew up under Roman rule and forgot Boudicca's rebellion. They accepted Roman culture as a birthright.

Boudicca was said to have taken poison rather than watch the destruction of her people. Legend says she died of shock after the battle. Another story has her torn apart by four horses at the order of Suetonius. Cassius Dio wrote that she was buried secretly with great honor, but no one knows where that may be. On Hampstead Heath, within a grove surrounded by a wire fence, many Britishers believe that this is the burial site. Bones and ashes are sometimes found there. Some say these are sacrifices to the dead queen by modern-day Druids or witches. Londoners, however, think her remains are under Track No. 5 at Paddington Station.

Tacitus wrote that with Boudicca's death, his father-in-law could then "bring civilization to this rude, scattered and war-like people." Towns with public baths were rebuilt. Villas with mosaic floors were introduced for wealthy Romans. Prosperity returned to Roman Britain, until other conquerors, Norse, Saxons, Normans, in-turn, joined the immigrations and, once again changed the face of Greater Britain.

As for Boudicca, there she is on the Embankment, commanding those who walk along the Thames, sword in hand, ordering London traffic.

SELECTED BIOGRAPHY

Collingswood, R.G. and Myres, J.N.L., *Roman Britain and the English Settlements*. Oxford: Clarendon Press, 1937.

Dio's Roman History. Vol. VIII. (trans. Ernest Cary).Cambridge, Mass.: Oxford University Press, 1961.

Dudley, Donald. *The Rebellion of Boudicca*. New York: Barnes and Noble, Inc., 1962.

Will Durant. *The Story of Civilization, Vol. III, Caesar and Christ*. New York: Simon and Schuster, Inc., 1944.

Gibbon, Edward, Esq. *The History of the Decline and Fall of the Roman Empire, Vol. I*. Philadelphia: Henry T. Coates and Company, 1845.

Ebert, Roger and Curley, Daniel. *The Perfect London Walk*. Kansas City/New York: Andrews, McMerl and Parker, 1986. Following directions in the book, a traveler arrives at Hampstead Heath and the hillside believed to be the burial site of Boudicca.

Encyclopedia Britannica. Vol. III "Boadicea." Chicago, London, etc.: William Benton, 1963.

Haverfield, Francis John. *The Roman Occupation of Britain*. (Six Ford Lectures). Oxford: Clarendon Press, 1924.

Complete Works of Tacitus Annals. New York: The Modern Library, Random House, Inc., 1942. When his works were rediscovered during the Renaissance, the world first learned of Boudicca and her rebellion against Rome.

GUINEVERE OF THE PICTS

"And Guinevere – call her not back again
Lest she betray the loveliness Time lent
A name that blends the rapture and the pain
Linked in the lovely nightingales lament . . . "

Frances Brett Young in
Sword at Sunset

Early invaders of Greater Britain from where?

Picts: Finland, Thrace, Lydia, Norway?

Celts: Britons, Welsh—Brittany

Norse: Norway, Denmark

Gaels: Ireland (called Scotti by the Romans)

Germanic Tribes: Angles, Saxons, Jutes

Normans: France

The oldest stories of Arthur and Guinevere are from Wales. They were set down from oral tradition during the dark ages when other parts of Celtic Britain were being overrun by Saxons. The Welsh kingdoms retained their independence for a longer period of time. The subject matter of chronicles and annals was not necessarily limited to Wales or to the Welsh, but here was a repository for writers during a troubled, changing period in British history. Later, during the Middle Ages, stories were read and revised according to the circumstances of peoples' lives at that time. Often they bore little resemblance to what had actually happened, but they were what people five hundred years later thought had happened, or what they wanted to believe had happened.

Since then more books have been written about Arthur and Guinevere than any other couple in history, although there are still doubts among historians as to their existence. The supernatural and mythological have been added to the stories making the reality doubtful. However, if there was a once and future king or Dux Bellorum or Comes Brittaniae whose name was Arthur, he would have had a queen, whose name was Guinevere.

Who is to say what is history and what is legend as the mists of time have shrouded Camelot?

The Meigle Stone

A twelfth century chronicler described the Picts as pygmies who "did wonders in the morning and the evenings but at midday lost their strength and hid in holes in the ground." By the time those words were written, the Picts had disappeared, along with the Britons of Strathclyde, into Scottish history. There was no one to dispute this unflattering description of them. Their language was lost; no documentary sources remained. Pictish symbols alone are found throughout northern and eastern Scotland. These Pictograms are unique, and are found mostly on commemorative stones. But no one has been able to translate them.

Historians speculate that the Picts were the first people to emerge from the tribal societies of the late Iron Age. From the fourth to the ninth centuries, they were dominant in northern Scotland. Then, as a people, they ceased to exist. Only standing stones with symbolic inscriptions remain.

There is such a unique gravestone in Meigle, Scotland. It is in the small, picturesque Meigle Museum, formerly a village schoolhouse. There are those who claim that this stone was taken from the burial site of Guinevere, King Arthur's queen. It was found in the center of the Strathclyde Valley, which was the heart of Pictland during the Dark Ages. If Guinevere existed, she would have been a Pict by custom, location, and symbol. The women of Meigle have chosen her to be remembered as their queen. They were not swayed by male historians of the Victorian Age, or by French chroniclers who wrote that Guinevere was a wicked, adulterous woman who brought down Camelot. They see her as a powerful, ancient warrior queen of the Dark Ages, beautiful, wealthy, and wise.

Who speaks for the historical Guinevere besides the women of Meigle?

After Camlann, Arthur's last battle, did Melwas, who was rising to power among the British kings, carry her off to Glastonbury? John Morris questions the background of Melwas/Meleagant. Did he have a Pictish grandmother? Is this why he fought Arthur and kidnaped Guinevere, taking her home to Pictland where she was buried with ceremony befitting a queen?

The Welsh Chronicles describe "a great Celtic king leading the fight against the West Saxons, who were pouring into England in search of land." Arthur, victorious at the battle of Mt. Baden, (c. 516) held back the Saxon advance for more than twenty years, depending upon which chronicle is read. He was seriously wounded or died at the last battle, (c. 537) on or near Hadrian's Wall, where the Roman fort of Camboglanna has been located.

Then, Geoffrey of Monmouth wrote *The History of the Kings of Britain*, (c. 1136) a medieval best seller. He has been called "the creator of the Arthurian legend." Few historians place great faith in Geoffrey who claimed to have based his information on "a certain very ancient book written in the British language" given to him by Walter the Archdeacon. Geoffrey's writings have often been dismissed as "strange, uneven and unacceptable as history." But is it possible that occasionally a little history peeks through the pages?

"Finally, when Arthur restored the whole country to its earlier dignity, he married a woman called Guinevere. She was descended from a noble Roman family and had been brought up in the household of Duke Cador. She was the most beautiful woman in the entire land."

Then Arthur held court with Guinevere at Caerleon. When the country was threatened by Romans in Gaul, he "handed over the task of defending Britons to his nephew Modred, and to his Queen, Guinevere." While Arthur was in Gaul, Modred "placed the crown upon his own head" and was living "adulterously" with the queen.

There is no mention of a Lancelot, only Modred. Arthur returned and fought his nephew and at Camboglanna, he died, so writes Geoffrey.

There is still no clear picture of Guinevere. Who was her mother? Where was her home? How did she arrive at Duke Cador's castle? Could she have been a hostage for the good behavior of the Picts? Why would Arthur want to marry her, despite Geoffrey's description of her "as the most beautiful woman in the land.?" Fifth century Britain was not a place where men married for love. It had a brutal, warring society where wealth and property meant power.

What could Arthur, usually classified as a Roman-Briton, gain by marrying another Roman-Briton? Above all, he was a political strategist; he had to be. Collingwood and Myres in *Roman Britain* write that he may have been the son of a good family, not necessarily noble. But Kathleen Hughes claims, "Arthur was born in adultery; what he gained was by violence." Or could it have been acquired by marriage? Was Guinevere a Pictish heiress whose dowry may have been the land of Sterling, gateway to the Highlands of Scotland, with its great round-rock mound about which knights on horses could easily gather?

In his *Chronicle of Scotland*, Hector Boethius discusses the relationship between Arthur and King Lothus of the Picts, or Loth of Lothian who had married a sister of Uther Pendragon, Arthur's father. Loth also had two sons, Modred and Gwain. When Uther died, Loth claimed sovereignty because the Picts had a matrilineal society; sovereignty descended through the female line. No Pictish king was ever succeeded by his son. Loth went to war with Arthur because of his claim to Uther's throne through his wife. When he was defeated, he demanded that the kingship should come to his line because Arthur and Guinevere had no children. The laws of Pictish society might explain Loth's attacks on the Britons in the south.

As the invasions by the Saxons and the Irish continued, Arthur needed the Picts on his side, or at least, a buffer zone in the north. The Northern Picts had a history of being fierce warriors. Tacitus credits them with holding the Romans at Sterling, and forcing them to build Hadrian's Wall and later the Antonine Wall to protect the Roman settlements.

He describes the Picts when they faced his father-in-law Agricola in the first century:

> They fought in the nude, adorned with iron; their bodies covered with tattoos of animals and symbols indicating their status in society. They used spears, swords and battle axes on the enemy.

Bronze or iron needles were used in tattooing as described by Charles Thomas in his article, "Interpretation of Pictish Symbols." Three hundred years later, these tattoo designs were used on stones for public display. With the aristocracy, the mirror and comb were used. In stories of Guinevere, the symbols indicate that royalty had passed that way. She has been described as having a tattoo of a crown on her hip.

After the Romans left Britain, the Picts built ships that sailed south to attack Britons. They sometimes rode small horses into battle. Lloyd and Jenny Laing wrote that they loved silver and wore silver chains as "symbols of power" before crowns. Guinevere would have worn silver clasps on her gowns decorated with symbols of comb and mirror. Dogs attended the deities and kings. It is possible that Arthur's dog, Cabal was a special gift to Arthur from Guinevere.

The French Romancers of the twelfth and thirteenth centuries further confuse the stories of Arthur and Guinevere, having little knowledge of Pictish society and the Dark Ages of Britain. "Courtly love," (look, but don't touch) a scarf lightly tossed to a knight before the medieval joust, would have had no meaning for the Picts.

In his book, *King Arthur: King of Kings*, Jean Markale accuses the French of taking Celtic epics, which they did not understand, and distorting them to fit medieval causes. He wrote that the Roundtable Romances "are barren dust heaps" the French writers made of them in "an attempt to impose Christianity on pagan myths." He denounces the story of Lancelot and Guinevere's love as "one of the silliest tales medieval literature has given us." He also claims that the original Celtic Guinevere was "a snarling bitch of a woman." (How did he know?)

Her name implies something quite different: white, beautiful, well-bred, white ghost, white spirit, purity or saintliness, according to Markdale and to Norma Goodrich. Could she have been a Druid priestess or a Christian? Was she converted to Christianity when St. Ninian made his home at Casa Candida or Whitborn Abbey and began converting southern Picts?

The venerable Bede, in his *Ecclesiastical History*, had some definite opinions about the Picts. He made a list of what he knew about them:

Sailed first to Ireland where they were not wanted, then to Scotland, took Irish wives;

Language different from Gaelic and Welsh;

Kings chosen through female line;

Came by sea from Scythia;

Converted to Christianity in 565 A.D.

A conversion to Christianity might have changed Pictish attitudes, but it would have taken time. Adultery was not a crime to them as it was among Celts or Roman Britons. A queen could take lovers if she chose. There is no evidence that Guinevere did or did not, but she had the privilege to do so. Maybe she did replace Arthur with Modred. There were no illegitimate children in Pictish society because all males were the sons of their mothers, i.e. Merlins. A twelfth century cleric probably could not comprehend this arrangement.

Guinevere of the Picts was not a lady reclining in her bower. Goodrich says Pictish women were often "captains of warrior bands." After their wedding, Arthur returned to battle. He was taken prisoner at Dumbarton Castle, where Guinevere, leading a war party, rescued him. She must have known the area well. If so, who held Dumbarton and "the red rock?" This was a time of shifting alliances, as Scotti (Irish), Norse, Saxon, and Britons fought each other for sovereignty. Could the Picts have had a temporary alliance with the Saxons? Where was Arthur's headquarters in the north? Where/what was Camelot?

A practical military leader, Arthur would have made use of remaining Roman encampments near the Roman walls. Carlisle, "the city of the legion at the western end of Hadrian's Wall, near the land of the Picts and the Scots" was well situated. Roman stables, baths, fortifications were there. Arthur could have more easily defended the land between the Antonine Wall and Hadrian's Wall. Several of the twelve battles fought by Arthur, including the great victory at Mt. Badon, which held back the Saxons, may have been fought in this area.

But, where was Guinevere's special place? Could it have been at Camelon, near Sterling, which was held by the Picts? It was located on the old Roman road going from York to Sterling, which would have made troop movements easy.

In a brief introduction to the excavation report of the Society of Antiquaries of Scotland, Boece is quoted as knowing that the remains of Camelon were Pictish, not Roman: "A little ancient city where the common people believe there was formerly a road for ships." Although in 1803, "the plough had almost leveled the banks" and the river was almost a third of a mile away. An anchor was found where an ancient river had formerly flowed at the foot of a steep bank, and "a great castle called the Maiden Castle" had been there. An alabaster vase, not of Roman workmanship, bowls with Pictish symbols of rabbits and leaping animals, a silver brooch, two long-handled combs "so commonly found in Scotland," were located at the site.

And the last battle, in which Arthur, Gawain and many Britons died, may have been fought nearby or at a Roman fort on Hadrian's Wall, Camboglanna. If Guinevere had been "living in sin" with Modred, as Geoffrey accuses her, and if Arthur had returned from Europe to reclaim his kingdom, it was in this vicinity that he defended his honor.

James Kenneth Campbell of Cambria County is certain that near another second century Roman fort, at the narrow bend in the River Irthing, Arthur was ambushed by Picts and Scots. Close to the small village of Arthuret, Modred, nephew of Arthur and son of his sister, waited to kill him. Somewhere in the north country, at Camboglanna or at Arthuret, the Welsh in their annals, believe this last battle was fought in a place "full of moss and marshes." This was Arthur's last stand, holding back the inevitable destruction of Roman-Briton civilization. Collingwood calls Arthur "the last of the Romans," and that "the story of Roman Britain ends with Arthur."

But after the battle, what happened to Guinevere? Most sources agree that Modred and his men raided Arthur's camp, carrying off his supplies, equipment, loot, and Guinevere. Did she go willingly?

If Modred died in the battle, his Pictish warriors would have taken her with them to the fortress at Dunbarre. There she was given into the custody of the Scottish king, Rion-Eugenius, Modred's ally. This could be the Urien to whom she had originally been betrothed before Arthur. Or she may have lived out the remainder of her life in a nunnery near Meigle.

After the loss of her husband, where could Queen Guinevere go to

41

be safe? To the southeast was Melwas/Meleagant who would probably kill her. To the southwest were the Saxons. The Irish (sometimes allies) were northwest, Anglo and Norse to the northeast.

The Pictish queen went home or was taken home to the heart of Pictland. And it is there in Meigle, Scotland that she is remembered.

• Author's note:

The Queen Guinevere, wife of King Arthur, selected for this book of *Wonderful, "Wicked" Women* was a person of unique gifts, not a mythical character. She was beautiful; she was a warrior; she knew she was a pawn in the brutal game of sovereignty among the small kingdoms of Dark Age Britain. She represented a dying race that joined with the Irish and the Britons of Strathclyde to form Scotland.

As for Arthur, reputable historians have written many books about him: who he was, what he did, where he lived. Many of them do not even mention Guinevere, his key to the north. All are highly speculative. Read them and be your own historian:

In Bede's, *Ecclesiastical History of the English People*, he describes the fifth century as a time when the Saxons "ravaged the land." Britain's leader at the time was

A certain Ambrosius Aurelianus, the sole member of the Roman race who had survived this storm in which his parents who bore a royal and famous name, had perished. Under his leadership, the Britons regained their strength, challenged their visitors to battle, and, with God's help, won the day. From that time, first the Britons won and then the enemy were victorious, until the year of the siege of Mount Badon, when the Britons slaughtered no small number of their foes about forty-five years after their arrival in Britain.

Could this be Arthur, or his father, or his grandfather, or a

42

capsulization of three members of one Roman-Briton family?

Geoffrey Ashe has discovered the Arthur of legend and of history in the person of Riothamus of Brittany. He writes that the tombstone at Meigle "actually portrays Daniel in the Lion's Den." Look at the picture; what do you see? Is it Daniel or a woman riding a horse, surrounded by her dogs?

However, there is still another King Arthur, writes W. A. Cummings in *King Arthur's Place in Prehistory.* This Arthur has a Stonehenge connection and possibly a Greek or Mycenaean connection or an Egyptian connection. Was Arthur the end of a "long line of kings in the Stonehenge Dynasty? A Bronze Age king?" Was this "sudden demise of Wessex culture," followed by the building of civil strife and hill forts? But where is Guinevere in this history?

Nennius wrote a *History of the Britains* in which there is a King Arthur, a "dux bellorum," a leader of battles with a war dog named Cabal, but no Guinevere.

Perhaps it is the ghost of Guinevere that haunts historians who want to believe in her existence.

"Most legends are rooted in myth. And legends live longer than truth."

Susanna Kearsley, in
Named of the Dragon

SELECTED BIBLIOGRAPHY

Alcock, Leslie. *Arthur's Britain*. Middlesex, England: The Penguin Press, 1971.

Ashe, Geoffrey. *The Discovery of King Arthur*. New York: Anchor Press/Doubleday, 1985. He claims that Riothomus is Arthur.

Bede's *Ecclesiastical History of the English People*. Edited by Bertram Colgrave and R.A.B. Mynors. Oxford: Clarendon Press, 1969.

Boece, Hector. *The Bulk of the Chronicles of Scotland*; a metrical version of the *History of Hector Boyce* by William Stewart, Vol. II, London: Longman, Brown, Green, Longmans and Roberts, 1858.

———. *Chronicle of Scotland, 1540 Number 851, the English Experience*. Norwood, N.J.: Walter J. Johnson, 1977.

Castleden, Rodney. *King Arthur, The Truth Behind the Legend*. London and New York: Routledge, 2000. He mentions Guinevere once: Modred attacked and took possession of Kelliwic "where he pulled Guinevere from her throne and insulted her." (?)

Collingwood, R.G. and Myres, J. N. L, *Roman Britain and the English Settlements*. Oxford: Clarendon Press, 1937.

Coughlin, Roman. *Illustrated Encyclopeadia of Arthurian Legends*. New York: Barnes and Noble, 1995. Picture of cairn with stone on top and paw print of Arthur's dog, Cabal.

Cummins, W A *The Age of the Picts*. Great Britain.:Sutton Publishing Limited, 1995.

———.*King Arthur's Place in Prehistory*, Great Britain: Alain Sutton Publishing Limited, 1992.

Eaton, David MacClean, *Was Queen Guinevere Buried in Scotland?"* Epigraphic Society Occasional Publications. Ed. By Barry Fall. Arlington, Mass., Vol. 18, 1984.

Excavation of the Roman Station of Camelon, VII. Account of the Excavation of the Roman Station of Camelon, near Falkirk, Sterlingshire by Society of Antiquaries of Scotland, Read March 12, 2000.

Geoffrey of Monmouth. *History of the Kings of Britain*. (Trans. Charles W. Dunn). New York: E. P. Dutton, 1958.

──────. *History of the Kings of Britain*. (Trans. Lewis Thorpe). Baltimore, Maryland: Penquin Books, 1966. Read for purposes of comparison.

Goodrich, Norma Lorre. *Guinevere*. New York, N.Y.: Harper Perennial, 1991.

──────. *King Arthur*. New York, Toronto: Franklin Watts, 1986. Following in her footsteps through Scotland and to the Isle of Mann made Arthur and Guinevere true sovereigns of the Dark Ages.

Henderson, Isabel. *The Picts*. New York, Washington: Frederick A. Praeger, 1967.

Hughes, Kathleen. *Celtic Britain in the Early Middle Ages*. Suffolk: The Boydell Press, 1980.

Kearsley, Susanna. *Named of the Dragon*. New York: Berkley Books, 1998.

Laing, Lloyd and Jenny. *The Picts and the Scots*. Dover, N.H.: Alan Sutton Publishing, 1993.

Markale, Jean. *King Arthur: King of Kings*. (tr. Christine Hauch). Paris: Gordon and Cremonesi, 1976.

Morris, John. *The Age of Arthur*. New York: Charles Scribner's Sons, 1973.

British History and the Welsh Annals. Edited and translated from the Latin by John Morris. London and Chichester: Rowman and Littlefield, 1980.

Sutherland, Elizabeth. *In Search of the Picts*. London: Constable and Company Limited, 1994.

Thomas, Charles. "The Interpretation of Pictish Symbols, Animal Art in the Scottish Iron Age". *Archeology Journal* CXVIII, 1961. (Published in 1963).

Turner, P.F.J. *The Real King Arthur: a history of post-Roman Britannia, A. D. 410-A. D. 593.* [Alaska] SKS Publications, 1993.

Wade-Evans, A. W. *Nennius's History of the Britons.* London: Society for the Promotion of Christian Knowledge, 1938.

Wainwright, F.T. *The Problem of the Picts.* Westport, Conn.: Greenwood Press, 1970

Meigle Museum, Scotland

ZENOBIA

"Her face was dark and of a swarthy hue, her eyes were black and powerful . . . her beauty incredible . . . "

Trebellius Pollio

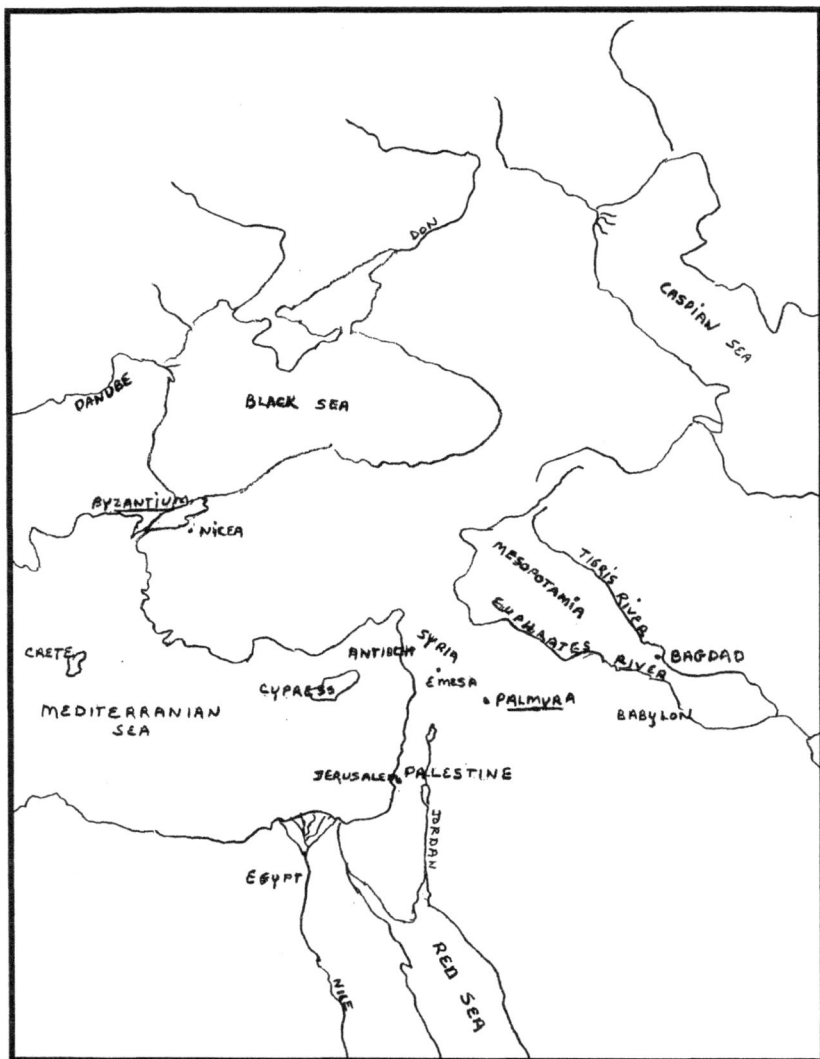

She moved as gracefully, but silently as the leopard she had been tracking. He was a mutant, all black. At dawn he was reclining on a tree at the edge of the desert, his tail moving slightly which was how she had finally spotted him. He was not an easy target, but she knew he belonged to her when he had not attacked first.

As she stood up and threw the javelin, all in one movement, he raised his head, looked at her and death; she awoke. The Roman night was warm and muggy. A moment before, the desert at dawn in her dream was deliciously cool. Did she miss the desert and her old life? Here was a staid, Roman matron, ensconced in a Tivoli villa overlooking the countryside, secure in prestige, still beautiful after child-bearing years, dreaming of her desert and hunting leopards at dawn.

As the Roman Empire continued to crumble in the third century, and no military assistance came from Rome, the city of Palmyra became virtually autonomous, there on the edge of a sea of sand. It had grown up by the spring of Efga, and became a favorite resting place for men and camels crossing the desert, bringing silks and spices from the Far East. "The place of palms, this Bride of the Desert" was a perfect connection between the Euphrates River and the Syrian coast for trade. The water from the spring made possible the palm trees for shade and the fruit for hungry travelers. Romans also had considered Palmyra to be a buffer kingdom for them at the edge of the empire.

As one corrupt and short-lived Roman emperor succeeded another, the King of Palmyra, Odenath, was forced to rely on himself to protect his city. He drove back the Persians in A.D. 262 and a reliable Roman Senate rewarded this uncrowned king with a title that meant "restorer," as he attempted to reestablish the majesty of Rome in the East. But did Odenath want more than an empty title? He ruled his desert kingdom.

Behind the monarchs were wealthy merchants who taxed the incoming goods of caravans before they were sent on to Rome. But there were also "warrior knights," as Richard Stoneman called them. The real wealth of Palmyra came from them. These were Bedouin tribesmen who "guarded" the caravans as they crossed the desert into tribal territory. A permit to pass as well as "protection money" was paid before the caravan could see the gates of Palmyra.

None of this was considered to be a challenge to Roman authority, although Odenath began minting some of this money with his picture as King of Palmyra. Just as he was emerging as a strong ruler, Odenath died under strange circumstances, along with his first-born son and heir. Then, Zenobia, his wife, took control. Edward Gibbon in *The Decline and Fall of the Roman Empire* is unusually complimentary to Zenobia. He attributes the previous successes of Odenath to her: "Instead of the little passions which so frequently perplex a female reign . . . the steady administration of Zenobia was guided by the most judicious maxims of policy." She gathered around her generals and intellectuals, including the Roman teacher and philosopher, Cassius Longinus, who was thought to be "a living library and a walking museum."

Zenobia's background is a mystery. She may have been a child of the desert, her father a great Ras. She may have been a Nabatean, or as Gibbon suggests in a footnote, Jewish, because she rebuilt synagogues and protected Jews within the Eastern empire. But she also protected Christians and was interested in studying Christian theology.

Zenobia claimed to be a descendant of Cleopatra and the Ptolemy line of kings who claimed Egypt after the death of Alexander the Great and his division of conquered lands. She wrote and spoke Aramaic, Greek, Latin and Arabic. Zosimus in *Historia Nova* credits her "with a man's mind and superior genius." Roman historians write of her as being "most lovely" and "possessing an attractive sweetness that far surpassed Cleopatra in chastity and valor." Iain Browning, writing in the 1970's, claimed her success was due to "repressed passions."

Her rise to prominence in Odenath's court is obscure. When she first appears, writes Agnes Carr Vaughn, she was Septimia Zenobia, second or third wife of Odenath and mother of three sons. As he hunted lions, panthers and bears, she may have ridden with him. When she becomes Queen of the East, she had one living son and heir, Wahballat; no one was left to contest her claim to the throne of Palmyra except the might of the Roman Empire.

Roman historians never accused Zenobia of plotting the death of Odenath. Only nineteenth century historians would decide that she just couldn't have taken over Palmyra and continued Odenath's plans for uniting the cities along the caravan routes without some evil plot on her part. The evidence is that she was devoted to Odenath and shared his dream for Palmyra. She had ridden with him into battle astride a white Nubian horse when her husband won back most of Syria from Persia, and reopened caravan routes. Odenath was then given supreme command in the east, including the Roman legions. He was elevated to the rank of *Dux Romanorum*. Zenobia would have done nothing to jeopardize his position.

She and her son were not present when he was killed in Emesa. Odenath, along with his son and heir, Herodian, and his nephew Maeonis had gone to a birthday party. Hunting lions was a part of the celebration and the men set out to flush a lion. The honor of the first javelin throw belonged to the king, but Maeonis was too excited at the prospect of a lion skin. He hurled his javelin first—and missed. He was chided for his breach of manners and ridiculed for missing the lion.

Another lion was located, and the riders went to hunt it down. Once again, more determined than before, Maeonis threw his javelin before Odenath. This time the nephew was taken from his horse and ordered from the hunt. The lion got away. Later, friends released Maeonis from the camp. He returned to the celebration claiming he had been wrongly dishonored; he killed Odenath and Herodian for insulting him. Odenath's men, in turn, killed him.

Zenobia and Wahballat, a minor at the time, were left to rule Palmyra. And Zenobia, as regent, did. When this happened, the Roman Emperor of the moment, Gallienus, became concerned about Zenobia's command of the caravan cities and the minting of coins in her name. He sent an army as a threat to her rule. Zenobia defeated it in battle. Then she took all of Syria. General Heraclianus returned to Rome in disgrace. So the generals assassinated Gallienus in Milan, not so much because of the defeat of his general, but because the people blamed him personally for the plague that crippled the Empire, his orgies, "his vicious life," and any other problems they had had. However, Gallienus was just one out of eighty emperors within a ninety-year period who were "mostly dissolute" and "stupid" according to Gibbon. Few of them died a natural death. In contrast to Gibbon, Treya Stark in Rome on the Euphrates gives a completely different view of Gallienus as a poet and orator who reorganized the armies. He was a good general, "tall, with curly hair and a thick beard, resolute, witty, well dressed, and generous." Who to believe?

With this poor record of emperors chosen by the generals and not the citizens, Marcus Aurelius Claudius was a surprise, especially when he appointed Aurelian commander-in-chief of the Roman armies. This satisfied soldiers who had fought with Aurelian against the Goths. Claudius II further set aside the previous decision of Gallienus to recognize Zenobia's son as King of Palmyra.

When her petitions to Claudius for recognition of Walballat were rejected, she took action, which again alarmed Rome. Zenobia wanted to control the eastern end of the Mediterranean Sea, so she decided to anchor her empire with Egypt.

First, she looked at her treasury and discovered she needed more money for a campaign. Her spies had informed her that officials had been skimming on taxes from the prostitutes guild, water rights, and salt. They were executed. Next, she learned the whereabouts of Claudius and Aurelian, hoping they would continue fighting the tribes of Western Europe.

As her revenues rose, Zenobia moved her troops to Emesa, to Antioch, and over the mountains to Tyana, the capital of Cappadocia. Before she took Tyana, she went to the oracle in Cilicia. The oracle warned her that Aurelian was "a falcon who makes doves tremble," implying the Palmyrenes were the doves and that Aurelian would make them fear him. This may have been bad news for her, but it did not stop Zenobia from her objective, which was Egypt. Marching at the head of her troops, she besieged and devastated Basrah, capital of Arabia. She took Lower Egypt. To celebrate her victory, she drank with her generals from golden goblets that she believed had belonged to Cleopatra.

Meanwhile, Aurelian defeated the Scythians and Vandals, returned to Rome, "nursed his vineyards, did the best for the currency, and rebuilt Rome's walls."

When news of her victories reached Rome, people demanded that Claudius save them from the woman who was defying the Empire. Would Rome be next? But Claudius was dying from the plague, and his brother Quintellius was waiting to become the new Emperor. Aurelian, the favorite of the troops, was not selected.

Quintellius ruled seventeen days, and then opened his veins. Meanwhile, Aurelian, still commander-in-chief of the army, had left his vineyards to fight and defeat the Goths in A.D. 270. His soldiers proclaimed him Emperor Lucius Marcus Aurelianus by tossing him up in the air in a blanket, which probably precipitated the suicide of Quintellius.

Now Zenobia, who called herself Queen of the East, had to come to terms with Emperor Aurelian. She still wanted him to recognize Wahballat as successor to his father. She even sent Aurelian corn from Egypt and minted a coin in his name. Again Zenobia waited. When there was no word from Rome, she proclaimed her son "Augustus," or Emperor. This was too much for Aurelian; there could be only one Augustus in a unified

Roman Empire. So the struggle began between Zenobia and Aurelian for control of the East.

The new Emperor was a complicated man. His biographer describes him as "comely, rather tall, strong, endowed with manly grace, though a little too fond of wine and food." Was he a cruel man? Probably. It was a cruel age. He permitted his soldiers to "loot and burn," but he was a strict disciplinarian with a code of conduct for his troops. This was most unusual. He ordered his officers to

Restrain the hands of your soldiers. None shall steal . . . let them control themselves in their lodgings with propriety, and let anyone who begins a brawl be thrashed.

Aurelian had great respect for Zenobia's fighting abilities. When Zenobia, after her five-year reign,was finally captured, Aurelian's soldiers wanted to kill her, but he thought that would be "improper." Humiliation, yes; but *death* to a courageous woman? No, even after she had defied him. She was a warrior, and he would not order her beheading.

At one point in his campaign against her, he was wounded. Gibbon explains that Aurelian had to write a letter to the Roman Senate to maintain their confidence in him:

The Roman people speak with contempt of the war I am waging against a woman. They are ignorant both of the character and power of Zenobia.

Aurelian then sent his best general, Probus, to Egypt. She lost Egypt to him and retreated back along the route of the caravan cities. Her allies in Arabia, Armenia and Persia had heard of Aurelian and the Roman legions, and offered her no support as he pursued Zenobia. Cities she had taken declared for Aurelian and closed their gates to her. She was forced to fight her way back to Palmyra where she hoped the desert and the Bedouin would defeat his troops.

Near Antioch, Aurelian waited for Zenobia's formidable cavalry. He warned his troops not to engage the Palmyrenes because of their horsemanship and heavy protective armor. Instead, he drew up his infantry across the Orontes River with orders to run when Zenobia's forces crossed the river. Aurelian thought that the burning heat and the heavy armor would exhaust her men and horses. Then he planned to attack. He was right. It was a terrible defeat for Zenobia, but the slaughter on both sides "stained the desert for months." Because he did not "loot and burn" Antioch, its citizens were prepared to supply Aurelian with food when he began his siege of Palmyra.

From Antioch, Zenobia withdrew in the night leaving the city to Aurelian, where he issued a general pardon. At Tyana, the Emperor saw the gates closed against him. It had given all its food to Zenobia. "In this city I will not leave even a dog alive." But when his troops took Tyana, the people had fled and they could kill only dogs.

Aurelian followed Zenobia to Emesa. On the plain in front of the city, before the attack, her troops fled. The gates of Emesa closed to her. Aurelian's tall, dark Palestinian troops with three-foot war clubs were used on Zenobia's archers before they could draw their bows.

On to Palmyra, across the desert Aurelian pursued Zenobia. There was no water for his troops. Zenobia, with the Bedouins, raided his camp at night; then disappeared. When he finally reached Palmyra after the tortuous trek, he was thirsty, exhausted, and furious. What did he expect from Zenobia, capitulation?

He began siege operations, which the Roman army had almost perfected in their wars across the Empire. He cut off her supplies. Food now came to Aurelian across the desert in convoys from cities he had taken, but had not plundered, like Antioch. He may have been cruel, but he understood public relations. The wealthy fled the city, many going into

Aurelian's camp. He bought off the Bedouins who had been Zenobia's main supporters.

As the siege continued, he wrote a letter to Zenobia:

From Aurelian, Emperor of the Roman World and recoverer of the East

"For I bid you surrender, promising that your lives shall be spared. . . . [Was her son Wahballat with her?] As for the people of Palmyra, their rights shall be preserved. "

Zenobia understood that everything she possessed would be forfeited: her horses (those uneaten during the siege), camels, and jewels, even her royal robes.

From Zenobia, Queen of the East, to Aurelian Augustus,

"None, save yourself, has ever demanded by letter what you now demand . . . "

The return letter was written in Greek, not Latin, the implication being that he was uneducated and needed a translator. Vopiscus said he was very angry and resolved to starve the city into submission. Huxley attributes the letter to Longinus, advisor to Zenobia.

Zenobia even sought help from Persia by offering herself to the prince whose father she had destroyed. Finally realizing no help would come, she fled at night from Palmyra, hoping to cross the Euphrates into Persian territory. But she was betrayed, and the Roman troops captured her a few miles from the river. Zosimus said the remaining citizens in Palmyra demanded the gates be opened to Aurelian. Her generals, Zabdas and Vorades, surrendered the city. Longinus and Nicomachus, her advisors, the generals, and Zenobia were taken to Emesa for trial.

Aurelian forbade his soldiers to loot Palmyra. His troops were determined to put her to death, but he wanted her for his "triumph" in Rome. After all, he was judge and jury, and all decisions were his.

At her trial, Zosimus and Gibbon both wrote that she claimed to have been "led astray" by her advisors, and that this is how she escaped death, while they were all beheaded. But Zosimus, a Roman with an attitude, wrote several hundred years after the trial, and Gibbon wrote more than fifteen hundred years later during the Victorian age. Nothing in her character and nothing in her relationships, neither with her generals nor with her advisors, would cause her to place the blame for her decisions upon them. Zenobia had always made her own rules and decisions.

Gibbon claimed that she purchased her life "by the sacrifice of her fame and her friends." He also writes that "female fortitude is commonly artificial, so it is seldom steady or consistent." What have we here? It might have been more honest if he had written that her beauty and presence awed Aurelian, and he wanted to exhibit his prize to Rome. Someone had to die, but it was not going to be Zenobia.

Writing three hundred years later, Malas of Antioch describes Zenobia on display in the hippodrome there. She is supposed to have been exhibited, then placed in a cage in a public place for three days. He may or may not be a good source.

What happened to her son? No mention is made of him after her retreat from Antioch. When the Roman army left Antioch after the trial, Zenobia never saw Palmyra again.

However, before Aurelian left Palmyra, he went to the temple of the sun god Bal and gave thanks for his victory. He carried home with him votives that he placed in a temple to the sun that he had built on Quirinal hill. Christianity had not yet become firmly rooted in Rome until Constantine declared it to be the religion of the Empire. The sun god was incorporated into the Pantheon and was worshiped by many across the Empire.

From Palmyra, Aurelian marched toward Europe with Zenobia and his spoils of war. Only Zosimus wrote that she died along the way by refusing to eat. Other captives drowned crossing the Bosphorus. However, if this were true, why has so much been written about the "triumph," a procession for the victor that only the Senate could grant, and the only time soldiers could bring their arms into Rome. This was a great victory march for a conqueror along the Sacred Way, approaching the Forum from the East. Larry Ball describes it as a "raucous" parade with prisoners, floats, signs, booty, and a slave holding a laurel wreath over the victor's head. Aurelian wanted handkerchiefs given to the people so that they could wave them to show their approval of his accomplishments.

But before he reached Rome, Palmyra rebelled again in A.D. 272. Aurelian had been generous in victory with the city, leaving only a garrison of six hundred to keep peace. He wanted a functioning economy with the caravans passing through the desert to Palmyra once again and bringing taxes to Rome.

This time the city was destroyed: "We have not spared the women, we have slain the children, we have butchered the old men, we have destroyed the peasants." The Bedouin fled into the desert.

Finally, in a letter to his commander Bassus, Aurelian ordered, "the swords of the soldiers should not proceed further . . . " Someone had to be spared to repopulate the city. But this did not happen. The proud city, once the center of the world's caravan trade, became a miserable village amid ruins of temples and columns.

Aurelian had his "triumph," described as one of the greatest ever held in Rome. His troops were dressed in new tunics and sandals. He wore a long white tunic, embroidered with palm trees and a shorter purple tunic. On his head was a magnificent crested helmet. Four stags with full antlers pulled his golden chariot.

According to Vospicus, there were prisoners, wild beasts, elephants, pennants of the legions, and representatives of sixteen conquered nations. Gibbon wrote that the "triumph" opened with twenty elephants, four royal tigers, 1600 gladiators, and a train of captives who were Goths, Vandals, Franks, Gauls, Egyptians and Syrians. Vaughn accuses Aurelian of harnessing the king of the Goths to his chariot and later "killing him with his bare hands."

Pollio included Zenobia: "And there came Zenobia too, decked with jewels and in golden chains. She was wearing gems so huge that she labored under the weight of them."

There were a few critics who muttered that it was "unmanly" to lead Zenobia in the "triumph," but it is doubtful that they ever had to face her across a desert battlefield. One cannot help but wonder what Aurelian's wife and daughter thought as they watched this beautiful woman in a long ceremonial robe of purple silk, with her arms and legs bound in gold chains fastened to a gold collar. She had difficulty walking, but her head was erect. Aurelian had permitted her to wear her helmet, which was described as "gilt with purple fillet, which had gems hanging from the lower edge, while its center was fastened with a shell-shaped jeweled center called 'cochlis'."

When the "triumph" was over and the crowds left the streets, what happened to Zenobia and Aurelian?

In honor of his new temple to the sun, Aurelian established in A.D. 274 the annual festival of the sun falling on the winter solstice, December 25. Then, when the empire became Christian, the birthday of Christ was transferred to this date. It made the new religion more acceptable to those who still enjoyed the festivities of the old religion of the sun, worshiped by Zenobia and accepted by Aurelian. Stoneman gives Zenobia credit for Christmas day although that might seem to be stretching her influence.

Aurelian was murdered in A.D. 275 by a trusted general who had joined a conspiracy. Gibbon calls the Emperor a "useful though severe reformer of a degenerate state."

What happened to the woman who called herself Queen of the East? Pollio wrote she lived "not far away" in a villa that belonged to Aurelian. Or did he build her a villa in Tivoli where "she lived with her children?" Who was their father? Did she later, after Aurelian's death, marry a Roman Senator and have his children? Gibbon writes that she had daughters who married into Roman nobility. Was Zenobius, Bishop of Florence, in the fifth century, a descendent? None of her biographers has an answer.

However, above all else, Zenobia was a survivor. She could have turned herself into a Roman matron, and lived her life in the final turbulent years of the third century, protecting herself and her children.

But in the hours before dawn, on warm nights when there was a hunter's moon, did she dream of Aurelian the conqueror, or did she dream of hunting leopards in the desert and of riding her camel into the dawn?

SELECTED BIBLIOGRAPHY

Ball, Larry F. "A Great Empire's Beating Heart." *Archaeology Odyssey*, November/ December 1999, pp. 29-39.

Browning, Ian. *Palmyra*. Park Ridge, NJ: Noyes Press, 1979.

Gibbon, Edward, Esq. *The Decline and Fall of the Roman Empire Vol. I*. Philadelphia: Henry T. Coates and Company, 1845.

Huxley, Julian. *From an Antique Land*. London: Max Parrish, 1955.

Rostovizeff, M.I. *Caravan Cities*. Translated by D. and T. Talbot Rice. Oxford: Clarendon Press, 1932.

Stark, Freya. *Rome on the Euphrates*. New York: Harcourt, Brace and World Inc., 1966.

Stoneman, Richard. "The Syrian Cuckoo: Rome and the Unconquered Sun." *History Today*. London: December 1988, Vol. 38, pp. 29-34. He credits Zenobia's sun god with Christmas day.

Vaughn, Agnes Carr. *Zenobia of Palmyra*. Garden City, NY: Doubleday and Company, 1967.

Zosimus. *Historia Nova, the Decline of Rome*. San Antonio, Tex.: Trinity University Press, 1967.

LADY HESTER STANHOPE

1776 – 1839

" . . . a nose that scorned the earth, shooting off, one fancies, toward some eternally eccentric heaven."

Lytton Strachey

Lady Hester Stanhope. *From the reproduction of a miniature by an unknown artist in the British Museum.*

Her family referred to her as "this strange woman." Women instinctively disliked her and the feeling was mutual. The Dictionary of National Biography lists her as "eccentric." George III admired her and told her uncle that she would be a "superior minister and a good general, too."

Lady Hester Stanhope was young, handsome and witty, but also prideful and arrogant. Lytton Strachey wrote that, "there was something wild and unaccountable in her temperament." Lady Hester probably would have agreed with all of these assessments of her. She was everything that well-bred English ladies were not.

At a time in Great Britain when a woman had few rights and no position in society other than her husband's, this unmarried woman refused to be imprisoned "by my own drawing room."

In this book, Lady Hester's story follows that of Zenobia because she went seeking the ruins of Palmyra which she said, "owed its chief magnificence to her (Zenobia's) genius. Lady Hester wandered through the Middle East especially in the areas controlled by Zenobia. She finally settled on a hill in Lebanon where she held court for travelers, refugees and visiting dignitaries.

When she died in June, 1839 at the age of sixty-three, some of her biographers have written that "it was a sad death, alone, penniless, half-starved, deserted by her servants." Ian Bruce said, "she died in rags and sordidness among squalling cats."

But Lady Hester, as always, had the last word: "I have no reproaches to make of myself but that I went rather too far."

It was an unusual family, and the childhood of Lady Hester Stanhope was also "different." She was the eldest daughter of Charles, the third Earl of Stanhope. His wife was the daughter of the great Lord Chatham, William Pitt. Her pedigree was perfect, but life at Chevening, the family home in Kent, was not.

Relatives describing the family have written that the lives of the daughters might have been different if their mother had lived, but unfortunately she died when Lady Hester was four. Mrs. Roundell, an early twentieth century biographer, wrote that the Earl disliked his daughters, but his sons by his second wife weren't treated too well either. The second son was apprenticed to a blacksmith; the youngest to a shoemaker. Lady Hester tended turkeys on the commons, while her younger sisters were turned over to nannies. His second marriage was to Louisa Grenville, a cousin to his first wife. The Duchess of Cleveland described Louisa as "stiff, frigid, chilling, more interested in fashion than in her sons or her step-daughters."

She later left the Earl, claiming that she was half-starved by the housekeeper/cook, who told Lord Stanhope that she was saving him money for his experiments.

The Earl called himself "Citizen Stanhope." He sympathized openly with the French Revolution and was ignored by the British aristocracy. This didn't bother him at all. He "ruled his household like a tyrant" and issued orders from his laboratory where he spent most of his time. Of course, he was a genius. He designed the first steamboat; he built the first calculating machine. But he did not believe in educating his children or in sending them to school.

Her father did not condone Lady Hester's first public appearance or "coming out," which was expected of young ladies of her class. So she rode off by herself to Lord Romney's review, a party given each year in honor of the king and queen. Unchaperoned, she entered English society with its pomp and pageantry. She loved it! The king was quite taken with her. Why hadn't he seen her before? She was much too attractive to be imprisoned in "Democracy Hall." George "Beau" Brummel admired her courage and her grace, and wrote to her that she was "charming."

Before she went to live with her grandmother, Lady Chatham, to escape "the slavery" of Chevening, she helped her older brother Mahon escape, too. She borrowed money to enable him to go to the University of Erlangen in Germany. The Earl, capable of "wild rages and violence," tried to find him, but Lady Hester kept the secret well. Her father never spoke to her again when she left Chevening. In later years, when she was desperate for money, Mahon forgot her assistance with his education.

Lady Hester's grandmother placed few restraints on her. She is remembered in 1800, age twenty-four, as "the intrepid girl who had been used to break-in her friends vicious horses for them." She loved horses and riding the countryside. When she finally reached the Middle East, Bedouins, especially, admired her as a fearless, magnificent rider. When she was dying there, she stabled her two "sacred mares," Leila and Lulu, who were fed whether she had food or not.

Lady Chatham died shortly after Lady Hester went to live with her. Where was she to go now? Lytton Strachey described her at this time, as being "very tall with a fair complexion, dark blue eyes. . . with something wild and unaccountable in her temperament."

Her uncle, William Pitt, took her in. He was not sure that this would be a good arrangement for either of them. His friends commiserated with him. However, it turned out to be a special three years for both Hester and Pitt, until his death. She took charge of his household, and he would become Prime Minister of Great Britain again, leading the government against Napoleon.

In January 1804, people in Great Britain believed the French were about to invade the island. Lady H. put herself in charge of the Light Dragoons and the Berkshire Militia, riding out along the coast to see if the French were coming and finding volunteers for coastal defense. At the house, she was his hostess, attentive to him and his guests. She made a park of the grounds where her rose garden still blooms. When Pitt returned to 10 Downing Street, Hester presided at the head of his table.

She had it all, but she could be arrogant and spoiled by his success. On one occasion she was rude to the Prince of Wales who could be a bore. She laughed at some of her uncle's colleagues and made fun of and mimicked George Canning, a future prime minister. He did not forget her.

At this time Lady Hester had an unfortunate love affair with Lord Granville Levinson-Gower. Joan Haslip refers to him of "the full mouth and limpid eyes," who had curling hair, a Roman nose, a career in gambling, and who "graciously permitted ladies to love him."

Levenson-Gower was "always pursued, never pursuing." His lover, Henrietta B., in a letter warned him about Lady Hester, "Is it quite honorable, dear Granville, to encourage a passion you do not mean seriously to return . . . ?" Of course, marriage was never considered by him.

Hester fell hard. She was infatuated, possessive, and demanding. At every party she would corner him. He soon "tired of his six-foot Amazon chasing him around," and "elegantly, he decamped." He left England for the ambassadorship in St. Petersburg, Russia. Hester became ill. It was rumored that she was pregnant. She isolated herself from everyone while she over-dramatically mourned her lost lover.

A defining time in her life was approaching. Pitt, never strong physically, became seriously ill and died. Hester had nursed him, cared for him, and was devastated at his death. She was now alone, without a protector, in a society that accepted only wealth and family. Hester had neither. Pitt understood what would happen to her and tried to prepare before his death. He had little money and both he and Hester, like many in the English upper class, were profligate spenders with money they did not have.

Pitt's last request before his death was that his niece be provided for. She was to receive £1500 a year and a small house. Parliament lowered this to £1200. Years later when Lady Hester was in debt and desperately needed money, the Prime Minister, whom she had insulted, and who was advising a very prim and proper young Queen Victoria, cut off her pension.

After Pitt's death, Lady Hester moved to the house on Montague Square. She tried to make a home for her half-brother Charles. With very modest means, little influence, and many enemies, she attempted to be circumspect at a time of royal scandals and corruption. Grenville relatives, whom she had called "broad-bottomed," and had slighted while she lived with Pitt, now pitied her. She hated this more than their compassion, which didn't extend to money. They offered her horses, but she had no carriage, a necessity for English society. She was isolated, and estranged from her father and older brother. When her half-brother Charles and a dear friend, Dr. John Moore, were killed on the continent at the Battle of Corunna, she left London for a cottage in Wales. At 33, she was unmarriageable and penniless. The Welsh mountains were beautiful in purple and gray, and she rode her horse daily into the countryside, giving away advice, medicines, clothing, and money she needed to support herself.   Martin Armstrong wrote that there was a "feverish recklessness" about her. She was driven "and she drove others." She tried farming and bought a cow, naming it Pretty Face. But she could not adjust to her radically changed position in society where she was no longer courted or consulted. She sold the cow and returned to London. Life seemed over for her.

When her remaining half-brother James returned to his regiment at Gibraltar, she left England with him, never to return.

Perhaps this is where her story should begin or end. What if her mother had lived to arrange a marriage with wealth and political power? What if Pitt had not died as a relatively young man who could have provided for his niece's future needs? What if she had lived a century later when her influence might have prevented wars or fomented insurrections?   In the early nineteenth century, she considered that she was left without options in England, so she left her country to make a home and a
reputation for herself in another part of the world.

Martin Armstrong, writing in *Six Brilliant English Women*, leaves Lady Hester for his last biographical sketch. He was extremely critical of her, perhaps he didn't like her:

She failed in the end to secure power, maternity or a man's love. She had a tyranny that claimed absolute subjugation. She gave much but she exacted much in return . . . she lacked self-knowledge and discipline.

Leaving her brother with his regiment in Gibraltar, she took off for Malta with her maid; a young Scot, Michael Bruce; Dr. Meryon, her

70

physician; friends, servants, guides, and guards. Dr. Meryon was from Oxford. He knew the classics but not much medicine. He learned while traveling with Lady H. and supported her always as she proceeded to do whatever she was advised not to do. In Malta she "contrived to affront almost all the women in the place." She began a scandalous passionate love affair with Bruce.

In May, Michael Bruce had met Lady Hester at a party. Michael found her "more agreeable, better informed, of extraordinary talent." In June, in the palaces of St. Antonio, they fell in love. Lady Hester wrote to Michael's father, Crawford Bruce, a wealthy businessman and a member of the House of Commons.

"You may have heard that I have become acquainted with your son, his elevated and statesmanlike mind, his brilliant talents to say nothing of his beautiful person . . . to know him is to love and admire him, and I do both."

She offered to "resign him, at some time in the future to someone worthy of him." He also wrote to his father about his affair: "Far from being ashamed, I feel most proud in openly confessing to you that I most seriously love and admire her."

Meanwhile, the father received an anonymous letter warning him of Lady Hester and her wild ways. Crawford then wrote to his son, " . . . it is a false system which builds on a disregard of the world's opinion."

Lady Hester cared little for the "world's opinion."

She visited the British fleet in overalls, a military great-cloak, and a cocked hat. Her old enemy at the British Embassy was "shocked" at her behavior, especially when she applied for a visa to visit Napoleon in France. He was at war with Great Britain. Lady H. called Canning a bigot for not granting her visa. He was, at this time, also minister to the Sublime

Porte in Constantinople, so that city was closed to her group. They sailed the Mediterranean Sea in a yacht belonging to the Marquis of Sligo while gossip followed in their wake.

In Athens, Lady H. and Bruce lived together openly. She wrote to her brother James of the arrangement, and he was furious. She also sent a note to General Hildebrand Oakes, governor of Malta. Although he did not approve of the liaison, he remained her friend.

Bruce offered to marry her and end the whispers about the lovers. She refused. He was spoiled and selfish, but he was one of the few men who stood up to her bullying ways. She knew he would not be faithful to her, (he was fourteen years her junior) and he was not. She was determined to take her happiness while it lasted, and never look back.

Another libertine they encountered as they sailed into the harbor near Athens was a naked Lord Byron diving into the sea. When Lady H. and Lord B. met on shore, they did not get along. His tongue was as sharp as hers. It was almost a competition between them as to who could be more outrageous.

In a letter to a friend, Byron wrote, "I saw the Lady Hester Stanhope at Athens and do NOT admire that dangerous thing . . . a female wit." She thought Byron "had a great deal of vice in his looks." The only good thing she could say about him was " the curl on his forehead." She noticed that "his eyes were set too close together."

The group did not remain long in Athens because Lady Hester was determined to get to Egypt. However, on the way they were shipwrecked off the island of Rhodes. A storm tossed them up on a small island near shore. Although they lost nearly everything, they were fortunate that they did not drown. Even a stray dog Lady H. had adopted in Athens was lost.

The ship's crew, not too sober during the storm, volunteered to take a small boat to the mainland for help. As the storm worsened, no one really believed the crew would ever return. In Dr. Meryon's account he wrote that they prepared themselves for death, but the crew did return after stopping at several taverns to fortify their courage. Hester had to be carried ashore when the boat capsized in the strong surf. She took money given to Bruce by his father to re-outfit everyone.

When Dr. Meryon returned from Rhodes with the outfit of a Turkish gentleman, Hester put it on and never again wore a dress. There was a freedom in wearing pantaloons with an over-jacket. She even shaved her head to wear the turban properly.

Traveling like a visiting Turkish dignitary, Lady Hester boarded a British frigate that carried the party to Alexandria. From there she went to Cairo for an audience with the Pasha who ruled for the Sultan in Constantinople.

For the meeting with the Pasha, she wore purple velvet trousers and a matching jacket embroidered in gold, a turban and a saber. The Pasha probably didn't know what to make of her, so in friendship, he offered her a pipe. Lady Hester did not smoke at this time, but she quickly accepted, and in later years, she kept pipes for special guests and for herself. She gave the Pasha a snuffbox and he gave her a white stallion, which Lady Hester sent to the Duke of York as a gift. It isn't known whether the Duke thanked her or not. Her generosity to everyone, rich, poor, refugees, sick, travelers, put her constantly in debt. She knew how to spend money she did not have, but she spent it so well.

From Cairo, she went to Jaffa where "a prophet" told that she "would visit Jerusalem, spend seven years in the desert, become queen of the Jews, and lead a chosen people."

Emily Morse Symonds described her entry into Jaffa wearing "a satin vest, a red jacket trimmed with gold lace, flowing pantaloons, all covered with a white burnoose." Of course the English residents were scandalized, but the people of Jaffa were impressed and poured coffee ahead of her as a sign of doing honor to this person. They did not know if she was indeed the Queen of the East (Zenobia returning) or the daughter of the great British ruler.

From Jaffa, Lady Hester traveled to Jerusalem from the north, through Syria, Caesarea, Acre, Nazareth to Sayda, where the Emir of the Druze entertained her. The Emir had recently converted to Christianity, to expiate his past deeds? He had blinded his nephews and had strangled his prime minister. Hester did not fear him. He gave her a horse so that she might ride in style into Damascus. Dr. Meryon wrote that, "the Emir was a very good man," who was captivated by Lady Hester, "who completely gained the hearts of the mountaineers . . . there was never a person . . . like her."

On to Damascus where native Christians were often persecuted in their quarter of the city and were not permitted to ride in the streets. Lady Hester entered the holy city at midday, dressed in her pantaloons, jacket, turban and saber, unveiled. People stood still in the streets and stared. Strachey wrote that the Bedouin "were overcome by her horsemanship, her powers of sight, and her courage."

In a drawing by R. J. Hamilton at this time, Lady Hester has on a turban with dark curls surrounding her face, pale skin, small lips, a pointed chin, large blue eyes and a rather long nose. How to account for the almost mesmerizing effect she had on men? She was overwhelming and she considered herself to be beautiful.

In 1813 she was making plans to pay homage to the memory of Zenobia in Palmyra. Some Arabs believed the English wanted to see

Palmyra because they thought it was their ancient traditional home. Michael wrote to General Oakes that he wouldn't be surprised "If she became a second Zenobia . . . Hester might even marry an Arab leader." The former lovers were obviously growing apart. Michael had enough of ruins and the people of the Middle East—he considered them to be "thieving and conniving." They didn't like him either. Finally, Lady Hester had come to believe that Michael would never achieve the goal of statesman that she had set for him. He was "uncouth and idle." His father Crawford needed money and Michael believed the only way "to travel was as a rich man." Lady Hester encouraged this lifestyle. But he also feared his father who was pressing for his son's return.

While Michael was in Alleppo, nursing a friend, Lady H. was planning to go to Palmyra. He was "injured" by her attitude of excluding him from her intention to go with or without him. It had always been her dream to see the ruins of Zenobia's beautiful city and she would make the journey her way. She arranged a meeting with "the great chief Mahannah el Fadel," and she conferred with those who knew about Palmyra. The road across the desert was not often traveled for fear of the Bedouin. It was a dangerous journey and she needed troops for protection.

Of the encampment of el Fadel she wrote that there were

> . . . the old poets from the banks of the Euphrates singing the praises of ancient heroes; women with lips dyed bright blue, and nails red, and hands all over flowers and different designs; a chief who is obeyed like a great king; starvation and pride so mixed . . . and I am Queen with them all.

Lady Hester made an agreement with the Bedouin to protect her, and she set out for Palmyra with her long-suffering physician, Dr. Meryon and a reluctant Michael. She dressed as a Bedouin, the son of a sheik. She seemed almost indifferent to Michael whom the Arabs thought to be arrogant. She ignored Dr. Meryon but he had gained some stature as a physician to the various courts along the way, although he had to guard his medical instruments for fear of thieves.

"I like my wandering life of all things," she wrote. I have a "large pair of yellow boots and a lance twelve feet long decorated with black feathers" and a tent guarded by a tall black slave whose "scowling looks and tremendous battle axe terrify everyone."

Leading the way, mounted on the Pasha's white horse with camels carrying tents, water and corn for the horses, Lady Hester sought the remains of Zenobia's greatness.

Iain Browning writes that her visit, "was all tied up with her sexual repression." It is obvious that he didn't like her, calling her "difficult and self-obsessed." Certainly she was difficult and self-obsessed, but hardly sexually repressed. But then Browning said the same things about Zenobia (see chapter III). The good Doctor Meryon who stayed with her throughout her wanderings over the years said,

> *Besides the wish to behold broken columns and dilapidated temples, Lady Hester may be supposed to have motives peculiar to herself . . . These columns and temples owed the greatest part of their magnificence to one of her own sex, whose talents and whose fate, remotely akin to her own, no doubt might move her sympathy so far as to prompt her visit to a spot which a celebrated woman had governed .*

Across the desert to the ruins of Palmyra went Lady Hester. The Bedouin prince, Naser attempted to intimidate her for more money by disappearing unexpectedly after telling her of an eminent attack by another tribe. Nothing intimidated Lady Hester. "Everyone take up your pistols," she ordered. "Move out." She was in her element. The Bedouin prince reappeared and she ignored him. Her plans for a grand entry into Palmyra had been made and nothing was going to delay her crowning as Queen of the East.

She entered the avenue of columns at Palmyra. Young girls danced beside her; some stood naked to the waist on pedestals throwing garlands before her; the Bedouins fired their weapons in celebration.

For this great occasion, she wore a bright red jacket, wide trousers embroidered in gold, her turban and the saber. At the great triple archway her turban was removed and replaced with a garlands of flowers while all the maidens danced before her. She later wrote, "I have been crowned Queen of the Desert at Palmyra." She called it "the greatest triumph of my life." Iain Browning called it a "pretty tatty affair," but he wasn't there. He also called her life a tragedy. She obviously did not think so.

Dr. Meryon and Michael remained in the background. After Palmyra, Michael Bruce's father requested that his son return to England and pursue "a respectable livelihood." Money was a problem and the passions of Lady Hester and Michael had cooled. When the plague broke out, Lady Hester insisted Michael leave the country. She also wrote to his father, "I fear he will end by hating me as I have teased and lectured him so much about taking more pains with himself. For God sake attend chiefly to his temper and his tricks." But when she wrote to Michael she said, "I shall never cease to pray for you . . . Adieu dearest, dearest, love. HLS."

In 1944, Ian Bruce went through two trunks sent to him from his mother's house and her garden depository. While reading the old letters, he recalled that his great grandfather traveled abroad with "some woman." Dr. Meryon had asked Ian's father for the letters, but the family did not wish to comply, nor did they want him to write about the love affair. Dr. Meryon wrote two books about his travels with Lady H. but never mentioned the romance. He served Lady Hester, did her bidding, prepared her way to Palmyra. She never thought to thank him. After twenty-eight years of following her, finding money to support her, taking care of her, all she could say of him was that he was "without judgment, without heart, he goes through the world, like many others, blundering his way . . . " She was not appreciative of friends.

Returning from Palmyra, Lady Hester got the plague in 1813 and almost died. The acting consul, John Barker, gave orders for her funeral, but she recovered. Dr. Meryon wrote to Michael Bruce in 1814 that she needed "bedding supplies and medicine." Michael was busy with other interests; he did not reply. On his way home, he "amused himself with a woman in Pera," and "occupied" himself in Vienna." Michael's name also was linked to that of Caroline Lamb, wife of Marshal Ney. While in Paris, Ian Bruce writes in *The Nun of Lebanon* that his great grandfather was honest with other women about his "guardian angel" in Syria. This must have been small comfort to Hester as she was recovering slowly from the plague.

From the Convent of Mar Elias where she was staying, Lady H. wrote to Michael: "Therefore it now stands that we never must live together again . . . " she signed it the Nun of Lebanon. She became more reclusive after sending the letter. Dr. Meryon noted this in his diary.

"In 1815, Michael wrote to his father of his 'arrangement' to pay Hester £600 out of his allowance." He felt "rather hurt" at "her abrupt way of communicating her intentions. She has become so completely orientalized that she will never be able to conform to the manners and customs of Europe." Crawford was in financial difficulty; he gave Hester £500 and her connection with Michael ended.

She planned one more adventure, to find buried treasure in the ancient city of Ascalon, where ongoing archeological excavations are taking place today. Lady H. had a manuscript given to her by a wandering monk. Based upon this, she planned an expedition. Fourteen days of useless digging produced nothing but a fine alabaster face, which she destroyed, not wanting hordes of English "looters" to steal the artifacts of Ascalon.

She assumed that the British Embassy in Constantinople would fund her search. After all, the Turkish government had given her supplies, "even providing a palaquin covered with crimson and ornamented with gilded balls." She was wrong about obtaining anything from the British government, and she was furious. Dr. Meryon wrote of her "fits of temporary madness," destroying every link with England in her frustration. He described "the dark, clouded look" in her eyes.

Her financial problems were overwhelming. She had continued to borrow from moneylenders who were only too willing to advance funds to the Queen of the East. When nothing was paid on the accounts, the British consul in Alexandria complained to London. Colonel Campbell recommended that her pension from Pitt cease until her debts were paid.

This was done. Now she had no money at all.

When Dr. Meryon left her service in 1817, he loaned her £100. She could not repay it. He had asked her to return to England with him, but instead, she moved to a larger complex in Djoun, where she spent the last eighteen years of her life. She complained that her home in the ancient convent at Mar Elias smelled because of the patriarchs buried in the walls. She had ridden out daily on her donkey, giving advice and spending time gardening and tyrannizing servants in Arabic. At Djoun, without money, she expanded her quarters, built a wall around it with an elaborate

terrace and rose garden. This is how she had always lived. Why should she change her lifestyle?

Back in England, her father, the Earl had died in December, 1817, leaving her nothing. They had not communicated in years. When her half-brother James committed suicide over his wife's death, he left Lady Hester £1500. This money was spent helping refugees fleeing the disintegration of the Ottoman Empire.

Before leaving Mar Elias in 1821, she had dug up for reburial, the remains of Captain Lousteneau, son of a French general. He had died of "acute gastritis" and had been buried in the rose garden. The captain had been an officer in Napoleon's Imperial guard. When he had arrived at Mar Elias, he had volunteered to care for the "sacred mares," Leila and Lulu. Lulu was gray and she was designated to carry Lady Hester into Jerusalem when she was crowned Queen of the Jews. Leila was chestnut, born saddled or sway back. After news of her brother's death, Hester never rode the mares again, nor did she leave Djoun after moving there. When the German Prince, Pucku Muskau, visited her Hester ordered him to visit the sacred mares. He said Lulu and Leila "behaved just like two old princesses obliged to grant an audience that bored them to death." After her death, the mares were sold at public auction, and unused to work or exercise, they soon died.

Lady Hester isolated herself at Djoun. However, she entertained travelers who came in deference to her "position." Some requested letters to the Bedouins to secure safety in crossing the desert. In 1827, Dr. Madden visited Djoun and called it an enchanted place and described Hester as one of the "few women who can boast more real genius and none of more active benevolences." Others described her as "a crazy old

80

woman," and Djoun " a lunatic asylum." The poet Lamartine described her as "the most interesting ruin in Lebanon." He was a disappointment to her because he paid more attention to his dog than to her. Alexander Kinglake stated, "Hester was absolutely sane."

She took up the occult, astrology, and studied magic. She believed the Messiah was coming and she would play a part in this great event. In Syria, the people referred to her as "the Prophetess," or the "Ancient Sibyl."

But there was no money. The ceilings needed repairs, the house was crumbling, the walls were propped up, and the furniture was falling apart. She was a gracious hostess to those admitted to Djoun, "always at twilight, so as not to show her wrinkles."

She still advised Pashas and travelers and was "revered by the people in bewildered affection." When Egypt overran Syria in 1832 and Acre was seized by the Turks under Ibrahim Pasha, she fed and protected wandering villagers. The Pasha ordered her to give them up. Of course, she refused. She defied her former friend Emir Beshyr, Prince of the Druze, calling him "a dog and a monster." She would not leave Djoun. She closed her gates and guarded them with an ancient Arab war mace. She built secret tunnels, "because events and catastrophes would come to pass."

When she believed the danger was over, she took to her bed and slept until late in the afternoon. Then she would get up, sit on a carpet, and smoke her long pipes, which might have caused her lung cancer.

Dr. Meryon arrived at Djoun in 1830 concerned about Lady Hester. He brought a wife whom Lady H. despised on sight; the feeling was mutual. The doctor was horrified at her poverty. He wrote that there were at least forty-eight old cats and kittens, caterwauling at night or whenever she raised her voice. He found the noise intolerable.

Lady Hester now wore rags, but clean rags. She told Dr. Meryon, "I should be what I intrinsically am, were I on a dung-hill." Her eyesight was failing; her teeth rotting. Dr. Meryon lasted four months, then he had to leave. He could not watch the decay. His wife rejoiced.

In her last interview with Dr. Meryon, Haslip writes that Hester sent him from the room on a small errand, then locked the door behind him and said that she would see him no more.

Hester knew she had to have money. In 1838, she wrote an almost demanding letter to the young Queen Victoria and to her Prime Minister Palmerston. They were indifferent to this "penniless, if autocratic, despot."

Now she was alone. There were no servants to berate. They had disappeared, taking anything saleable. She was sick, cold, and hungry in a house crumbling around her. Finally, she sent to Beirut for a doctor. The British consul, with an American missionary, Reverend W. M. Thomson, galloped to Djoun to find the house "absolutely silent." They lighted the lamps and passed through the courtyard to her room. Virginia Woolf wrote that in death she looked "composed and placid" on her dirty, tapestry-covered bed. They hired some workmen to help them dig her grave that night in a corner of the rose garden. The men found where she had interred the remains of Captain Lousteneau. Lady Hester had wanted to be buried beside him. To provide light for the workmen and for themselves, the two men placed candles in the empty eye-sockets of the dead Frenchmen, writes Ian Bruce. That must have been an eerie scene. Placing a Union Jack over a plain wooden box, Lady Hester was lowered into the soil of Lebanon.

The Reverend said a few prayers, adding that "she was wholly and magnificently unique."

The destruction of her home at Djoun was rapid and complete. Villagers took whatever was useful. The rose garden was plowed under. In 1912, the family tried to find her grave and to place a small monument there. It had disappeared.

When Dr. Meryon began writing the memoirs of his travels with Lady Hester, the Earl of Stanhope and his niece, the Duchess of Cleveland, both objected and refused to meet with him. He also approached the family of Michael Bruce for copies of letters between Michael and Hester. Of course, he was refused, so he wrote several books from years of notes he had taken along the way.

Since he was the only person who had tried desperately to help her through the years and had tried to be her friend, Dr. Meryon should have the last word on the life of Lady Hester Stanhope:

"Peace be with her remains, and honor to her memory."

SELECTED BIBLIOGRAPHY

Armstrong, Martin. *Six Brilliant English Women*. London: Gerald Howe, Ltd., 1930. Armstrong includes Lady Hester Stanhope; is very critical of her.

Browning, Iain. *Palmyra*. Park Ridge, N. J.: Noyes Press, 1979.

Bruce, Ian, editor. *The Nun of Lebanon*. London: Collins, St. James Place, 1951. Bruce is the great grandson of Michael Bruce. He found letters from "some woman" that had been kept in his mother's house and edited them.

Duchess of Cleveland. *The Life and Letters of Lady Hester Stanhope by Her Niece*. London: John Murray, Albemarle Street, 1914.

Encyclopedia Britannica. Vol. 21, p. 312. "Lady Hester Stanhope." William Benton. Chicago, London, 1963. Unflattering.

Haslip, Joan. *Lady Hester Stanhope*. New York: Frederick A. Stokes Company, 1936. A more balanced account of Lady Hester's life.

Meryon, Dr. Charles Lewis. *The Memoirs of Lady Hester Stanhope: as related by herself in conversations with her physician*. London: Henry Colburn, 1845.

————. *The Travels of Lady Hester Stanhope: narrated by her physician*. 3 Vols. Salisbury: 1846, reprint, Gordon Cremonesi, 1975.

————. *Travels of Lady Hester Stanhope: Romantic Reassessment*, editor, Dr. James Hogg. Salisbury, Austria, 3 vols. 1983.

Roundell, Mrs. Charles. *Lady Hester Stanhope*. London: John Murray, Albemarle Street, 1909.

Smith, George Barnett. *Women of Renown, Nineteenth Century Studies*. Freeport, New York: Books for Libraries Press, reprint 1972.

Strachey, Lytton. *Books and Characters*. New York: Harcourt, Brace and

Company, Inc., 1922.

Symonds, Emily Morse. *Little Memories of the Nineteenth Century.* Freeport, New York: Books for Libraries Press, reprint 1969.

Vaughn, Agnes Carr. *Zenobia of Palmyra.* Garden City, New York: Doubleday and Company, Inc., 1967.

Watney, John. *Travels in Araby of Lady Hester Stanhope.* London: Gordon Cremonesi Publishers, 1975.

Woolf, Virginia. *Books and Portraits,* edited by Mary Lyon. New York and London: Harcourt, Brace Javanovich, 1977.

THEODORA

Empress of Byzantium

"Theodora of the Brothel."

John, Bishop of Ephesus

Byzantium, the name of the ancient Greek city on the shores of the Bosphorus, evokes romantic and mystical imaginations of the Middle East. Constantine the Great built a new city on top of the old one there in A.D. 330 and made it the power center of the vast Roman Empire. However, two centuries later, the Empire was crumbling.

When Justinian, the Thracian peasant from the mountains to the west, came to power after his uncle's death in A.D. 527, Ostrogoths controlled Italy; Vandals were attacking Roman forts in Africa; Visigoths ruled in Southeastern Spain, while Slavs and Bulgars were pushing into the Balkans.

Justinian, known to history as a conqueror, lawgiver, and builder, dreamed of reuniting the Roman Empire and insuring Christianity as the religion of the state. He wanted to rule in the tradition of the Caesars. But there were insurmountable problems facing Justinian, beginning with his capital Byzantium/Constantinople. Although Greek was the common language, Robert Browning describes the million in population as "motley," with Illyrians, Copts, Armenians, Jews, Goths, and descendants of Hittites, Lydians, and slaves from everywhere crowded together in the center of the city. There were extremes of wealth, frequent riots and "bread and circus" control of the people—a volatile situation.

Standing beside Justinian and supporting him in all his endeavors and attempted reforms, was the Empress Theodora. Born into poverty, surviving by prostitution, she was Justinian's faithful, protecting consort.

"One who puts on the purple may never take it off," declared Theodora. And she never did, not even in death.

Theodora never denied her past; she never discussed it either. She took care of her family and those who had befriended her along the way. She never forgot those who challenged her or those who made her feel threatened. She reacted impulsively and sometimes violently against them. She was a great empress whose critics called her "extraordinarily fascinating, absolutely corrupt," courageous, audacious, complex, baffling, intense, proud, charming, perceptive, provocative, witty, vindictive, and cruel. Justinian adored her.

Theodora came as a child to Byzantium with her parents and sisters. She was the youngest of three daughters. The family may have arrived from the island of Cypress, or the Syrian mainland, or on a tribute ship from Egypt carrying grain to Byzantium. She is described by Charles Diehl in *Byzantine Portraits,* as "small and graceful with a delicate face, a thin, straight nose, beautiful black eyes under heavy brows." The few remaining mosaics of her show these features, especially the arresting eyes.

The family belonged to a small corps of professional performers. Her mother was an actress, which meant she was also a prostitute, and her daughters were destined to become prostitutes because the classes and jobs were hereditary and defined by law. Before Justinian could marry Theodora, he would have to change the law, which he would do. Her father, Acacias, was a trainer of wild animals who was hired by the Green Faction in Byzantium to keep the bears fed so they would not appear listless when on display between chariot races in the Hippodrome. The Greens and the Blues were the two officially recognized racing clubs.

The Hippodrome was the decaying center of Byzantine life, where emperors were crowned and where they spent money to satisfy the city crowds who came for the games, gambling, and politics. Theodora spent her childhood underneath the stands, near the menagerie where Acacias cared for the bears. James W. Vandercook describes her life as "weary poverty" in the dark, dank confines of the Hippodrome.

When Acacias died, his wife and children were left destitute. William Gordon Holmes wrote that the mother then tried "to unite" with her late husband's successor of the Green Faction, but another candidate bribed the "master of the shows," and the job was lost.

What to do? She dressed her daughters and placed flowers in their hair and around their necks and pushed them into the Hippodrome between races as "suppliants" pleading for work. The oldest daughter, Comito, was probably no more than seven or eight at the time. The members of the Green Faction in the stands, laughed at the children who were crying and holding each other in the center of the large racetrack. To embarrass the Greens, the Blues said they needed a bear-keeper too, and found quarters for the family on their side of the Hippodrome. The mother and children survived with the new bear-keeper of the Blues.

As soon as she came of age, (about twelve) Comito became a *hetaera*, linked to the theater, but in actuality, a prostitute, and a very successful one. The family moved from the basement of the Hippodrome. When she went out, her youngest sister, Theodora, carried a folding chair for her, dressed as a young slave in a very short tunic. The sisters became separated at a party one evening and in the dark, Theodora was picked up, taken to a brothel and sold to the owner. For several years she was held there and never permitted to leave the premises. This experience explains her later influence on many of the laws in the Justinian Code, which pertained to women. Robert Browning wrote that when she felt her position was secure in the palace, she summoned all brothel owners in Byzantium and lectured them on their evil ways. Then, she paid the owners the price they had paid to the parents for every under-aged girl, gave the girls new dresses, and sent them home.

She never forgot her escape from the brothel, but she was not trained for anything except prostitution and the theater. She was a born mimic who could read and write several languages. So she joined a theater group in Byzantium where she became a "burlesque comedienne, provocative and ingenious in dispensing with her clothes."

Most of the scurrilous information about Theodora, especially her life in the theater, comes from *The Secret History of Procopius*, printed long after his death. If the book had been seen in his lifetime, Theodora would have had him tortured, then strangled. Procopius was a Greek historian who belonged to a provincial hereditary, senatorial aristocracy. He became disillusioned with Justinian's attempt to restore the glory of the Roman Empire. When Justinian built churches and fought barbarians, this increased taxes for the landowners, and Procopius felt betrayed. His anger blazes forth in his *Secret History*. He describes Justinian as cruel, hypocritical, "a liar always, a faithless friend . . . insane for murder and plunder." He even blamed Justinian for floods, plagues, and earthquakes.

But for Theodora, he saved his most damning statements. It could be assumed from his writing that he, not Theodora, was sexually repressed.

"The girl had no shame," and certainly no lack of energy, if one believes Procopius. She was so young when sold, the brothel prepared her to act as a male prostitute. So Procopius wrote, "She attained the age of womanhood, in all the excesses of lasciviousness. . . . At orgies of the dissolute, she was the life and soul of the festivities . . . She was an instructress in depravity." He went on to describe in detail her activities.

"And toward her fellow actresses, she was always very bitchy . . . " and on, and on. In the theater, Theodora did an interesting tableau as a swan covered lightly with rose petals. Of course, the slightest breeze blew off the rose petals and she appeared without, which delighted the male audiences. She was very popular, Diehl says, "She amused, charmed, and scandalized Constantinople."

Edward Gibbon, in *The Decline and Fall of the Roman Empire* echoes Procopius. He certainly was not a contemporary of Theodora, but he, too, was critical of her, accusing her of driving a lover from her bed, if a wealthier favorite wanted her services. She was "avoided by all who wished to escape scandal or temptation."

This famous "pontifical" historian was accused by another historian of "setting down the right facts with the wrong inferences" and relying too much on the rage of Procopius. Even Procopius admitted she "had a lovely face . . . she was short and pale . . . handsome, and in all other ways, attractive."

What she needed was a patron to support her. She believed she had found one in Hecebolus, an official appointed governor to Pentapolus, a minor province in North Africa. She went with him, but after their arrival, something happened to the relationship. She may have become pregnant. Hecebolus threw her out of his house without money, clothes, or means of travel. She walked the southern rim of the Mediterranean Sea, prostituting herself for food or employment. Procopius wrote, "There is no city in Asia where she did not offer her body for pay." She was determined to get home to Constantinople. In Alexandria, Egypt she was befriended by a Christian group of Monophysites, who believed in one, single, composite nature of Christ, partly divine, partly human. She had become ill. Again, was she pregnant? Harold Lamb wrote that she had a daughter in Africa. Was that a reason for her dismissal from Hecebolus' house? Diehl also questioned if she had a son when she was young. Procopius said she did and that his father took him to Arabia. Did she have a grandson that she brought to her second palace in Hieron to protect him from the plague? There is no evidence for any of this, only speculation.

However, while in Alexandria, the Monophysites did take care of her. Later, when they were considered heretics, as Empress, she protected and befriended them without telling Justinian. She seems to have had a spiritual conversion in Alexandria, because upon her return to Alexandria, she was a different woman. She never returned to the "old life." She occupied a small house near the Palace where she sat silently in the doorway spinning wool; thin, intense, waiting.

In the evening, after working half the night, Justinian usually walked with an associate or a guard through the sleeping city. He was a lonely man, and people meeting him in the dangerous streets called him "protector." At the Palace he was really "associate" emperor to his uncle Emperor Justin, an illiterate military man who had brought Justinian to Byzantium with him. Justinian did all the paperwork necessary in running an empire, and he did it well without becoming a threat to Justin.

When he met Theodora one night as she sat spinning, he was probably forty years old to her twenty-six. Procopius describes him physically as being of "medium height, a little stout, his face was round and not unhandsome." Even her enemy Procopius wrote that Theodora was "strikingly beautiful." Justinian stopped to talk to her. A prostitute was worth more if she were intelligent and could speak several languages. Theodora had traveled, too; she had studied with holy men in Alexandria. And she knew men.

Justinian was intrigued, then "he was madly in love." One evening they walked back to the palace together and Theodora never returned to the small house or to her loom.

In all their years together, she was never unfaithful to him, and no scandal was ever connected to this area of her life. He not only made her his mistress, but he married her. For this, he had to ask the Emperor to change the law. Patricians were forbidden to marry beneath them, and by virtue of his position in the palace, Justinian, a senator, was a patrician. This is ironic because there was no law or procedure for succeeding to the throne of Byzantium. Anyone with sufficient military backing and a good sense of timing could become emperor and his wife would then become empress. Women from every walk of life could wear the crown jewels and the robes of royalty for a time. Princesses, tavern girls, village girls and peasants were all crowned by their husbands. And then there was the unmarried Theodora who had been a *hetaera*.

While waiting for Emperor Justin to make a decision to elevate Theodora, she slipped into seclusion. She was not permitted in the palace gardens, so Justinian gave her a house of Hormesdas where they lived together. There he became well groomed, grew a mustache, led parades, provided lions and leopards for games at the Hippodrome. The cold, lonely man took over many tasks for the ailing Emperor Justin, who was grateful. "By will of my people, I appoint my nephew and adopted son Justinian to be emperor with me."

The law was changed by Justin; the Patriarch approved of the wedding, after Theodora, shy, modest, and almost demur, appeared before him. Only Euphemina, Justin's wife, refused to accept Theodora's new status. When she died in A. D. 524, Justinian immediately married Theodora. She left her reclusive life. Public sentiment was with the couple because Theodora was a child of the streets of Byzantium. She appeared before the cheering crowds beside Justinian in violet-purple trimmed with cloth of gold, and her dark hair covered with pearls.

When Emperor Justin died in A. D. 527, Justinian I was proclaimed Emperor of the Romans with Theodora by his side. At the coronation ceremony, Theodora, too, received the oath of allegiance. From the beginning, this was a partnership. During the twenty-one years as Justinian's consort, Theodora was involved in everything from religion to the writing of the Justinian Code. She also saved his throne during the Niki riots when he almost lost everything—including his life.

In A. D. 532, there was general dissatisfaction in Constantinople. There was little money in the treasury for bread and games, because Justinian was planning his wars in the west against the barbarians pressing Rome. There was no wine for the harvest festival; no silver coins on the eve of the nativity to give to the poor attending church services. And there was a new tax on bread, with money going to a building program. Justinian's taxman was John of Cappadocia who was hated by everyone and blamed for everything. Procopius called him "the greatest scoundrel in the whole world." Theodora wanted him dead. She accused him of slandering her to Justinian when he tried to curtail her spending. He always set aside large amounts for himself, which he didn't bother to discretely hide.

The mood of the city was ugly. Blue and Green factions roamed the streets when there were no races planned in the Hippodrome. They joined forces to complain about the economy. Merchants and artisans were generally of the Greens, while farmers and landowners were Blues, so everyone was involved. The roaming groups came together as a mob and began burning sections of the city. The Senate went up in flames.

The great church Hagia Sophia burned. The Palace was besieged, but General Belesarius, Justinian's military commander, and his personal troop of Goths, drove back the mob and barricaded the streets around the Palace.

Theodora understood the throne was now at stake. She urged Justinian to appear before his people in the Hippodrome.

On a Sunday morning in robes of state, he faced the mob. He appealed to the people to go home, that John would be fired and reforms made. Harold Lamb wrote that they shouted back at him, "You lie, you swine." Justinian retreated back to the Palace. He probably did not realize how fortunate he was that no leader emerged to take control. The mob shouted out names of men to replace Justinian, finally deciding on Hypatius, a nephew of the late Emperor Anastasius. He did not want to be emperor, but the mob carried him to the Hippodrome against his will and crowned him anyway.

It looked like Justinian had lost. He even ordered ships to carry Theodora, the Byzantine treasure, and his servants to Thrace.

Theodora had been silent until then. She had never openly— nor in his councils—given Justinian advice. Several historians have quoted her words on this time of disaster:

> But that one who has been an emperor should become an exile, I cannot bear . . . As for me, I like the old saying that purple is the noblest shroud.

She suggested a plan by which Belisarius and the "barbarian Goths" would go through two partially hidden gates leading to the Hippodrome from the palace and attack the rabble before they knew the German mercenaries were there. Narses, an advisor, general and a eunuch who had supported Theodora, guarded the other gate.

A blood bath took place in the Hippodrome that Sunday. At least 30,000 citizens of Byzantium died in the afternoon; no one was left alive in the Hippodrome. The spectators' benches were covered in blood. Narses killed those who tried to escape through the gate he was guarding. Hypatius was brought before Justinian. He groveled and pled for his life. Justinian almost pardoned him because he had been forced by the mob to appear before it and be crowned with a makeshift wreath. Theodora said no. He was killed and his body, with that of his brother, was thrown into the sea.

After the Niki riot, Justinian became more autocratic, and Theodora never trusted the city and its people again. Justinian did away with spies and beggars and began restoring the city. But civilians could no longer bear arms. Theodora kept her "informants." Browning wrote, "There was a new, hard brilliance to Theodora . . . she now wore sapphires to match the pearls of her headdress."

She had no scruples when it came to protecting Justinian and the throne. Belesarius seemed to be gaining too much popularity with the people, especially after his successes in battle and honors bestowed upon him by Justinian. He was stripped of money and land and sent into exile on flimsy evidence, probably planted by spies of Theodora.

"To the western clergy she was a destructive schemer; the eastern clergy claimed her as a revered patroness," writes Lamb. She deposed a Pope and "put a scoundrel in his place." Joseph McCabe accused her of having had a Gothic queen strangled because of jealousy. "Many of these things were unprovable but not improbable." She had become a master of political intrigue.

When Justinian deposed Patriarch Anthemius for agreeing with the eastern confession of faith and sent the old man into exile, Theodora hid him in her chambers for many years, just as she had hidden other Monophysite clergy. For the Jewish people she instigated the return to Jerusalem of the temple candelabra and other treasures seized by Titus and taken to Rome.

After Trebonius completed the Justinian Code, new judges were appointed to hear cases brought by petitioners. Those women who thought they could not receive justice from the courts appealed directly to Theodora. She was known to take action on her own.

There are specific laws in the Code which seem to reveal the interests of Theodora in protecting women:

A daughter had equal rights with a son in the matters of inheritance.

A woman retained her dowry after her husband's death.

The child of a woman slave need not be a slave.

Women were enfranchised and had rights in divorce cases.

Women could hold property in their own names.

For the sixth century these were enlightened ideas.

However, Justinian became more imperious after Niki and imposed rigid protocol to define his rule. Members of the Senate were required upon entering the rulers' presence "to prostrate themselves on the floor . . . holding their hands and feet stretched far out, they would touch with their lips one foot of each before rising," writes Freya Stark in *Rome on the Euphrates*. There was fear of assassination. More money was needed to continue to rebuild the destroyed city. A defense against Persian aggression had to be considered and the barbarians were attacking Roman outposts in Africa.

In A.D. 548, Theodora became ill. She would have been reluctant to tell Justinian because he was totally absorbed with the rebuilding of Hagia Sophia.

When it was evident that she was dying, probably of throat cancer, he never left her side. He called her "his gift from God." She did not want to be moved to more comfortable quarters; she wished to die in the Palace of Byzantium where she had ruled.

At her death she was dressed in robes of state, the royal crown upon her head. On her feet were "red shoes embroidered with white pearls." Her body was placed in the nave of the Church of the Holy Apostles. The Pope of Rome, patriarchs, bishops, senators, ministers of state, and the people of Constantinople passed before her bier in respectful silence.

Justinium was "demoralized and isolated by her death." He dismissed his guards at night. He turned to theological studies. He decided to promulgate a decree ending persecutions of the Samaritan churches of the East for following ancient rituals. He desperately missed her. He was a lonely, old man whose later years were marked by misfortune. He must have known his vision of a restoration of the Christian Roman Empire was not possible.

Whenever he was in a procession passing by the Church of the Holy Apostles, he would stop, go inside, light candles and pray. He wanted to be buried next to her. At the Christmas procession that escorted Justinian to the dedication of a repaired Hagia Sophia, he added verses for recitation:

The luster of her hair,

The whiteness of her skin is gone.

But-oh, her eyes are shining.

Justinian died in A.D. 565. The bear-keeper's daughter and the peasant from Thrace were once again side-by-side, somewhere in the ruins of Byzantium/ Constantinople under the debris of 2000 years. Turks, Crusaders, Persians, infidels, heretics have marched and fought over their remains somewhere in the one time capital of the world.

Truly, their deaths marked the end of an age.

SELECTED BIBLIOGRAPHY

Barker, John W. *Justinian and the Later Roman Empire*. Madison, Milwaukee, and London: The University of Wisconsin Press, 1966.

Browning, Robert. *Justinian and Theodora*. New York: Praeger Publishers, Inc., 1971.

Diehl, Charles. *Byzantine Portraits*. Translated by Harold Bell. New York: Alfred A. Knoph, 1927.

Gibbon, Edward, Esq. *The History of the Decline and Fall of the Roman Empire*, Vol. III. Philadelphia: Henry T. Coates & Co., 1845.

Holmes, William Gordon. *The Age of Justinian and Theodora*, 2 Vols. London: G. Bell and Sons, 1912.

Justinian. *The Institutes of Justinian*. London, New York: University Press, Aberdeen, 1948. Lib. I, Tit. X; De Nuptüs, Tit. XXI. English introduction, translation and notes in Latin.

Lamb, Harold. Constantinople, *Birth of an Empire*. New York: Alfred A. Knoph, 1957.

———. *Theodora and the Emperor*. Garden City, New York: Doubleday and Company, 1952.

McCabe, Joseph. *The Empress of Constantinople*. London: Methuen and Co. Ltd., 1913.

Procopius. *History of the Wars, Secret History, and Buildings*. New York: Twayne Publishers, Inc., 1967. Translated from the Latin. Special arrangement with Washington Square Press.

———. *Secret History*.* Translated from the Latin by Richard Atwater. Ann Arbor: University of Michigan, 1961.

*Author's note: Two translations were used to be certain that every "infamous and scurrilous piece" of information was given its proper weight.

Stark, Freya. *Rome on the Euphrates*. New York: Harcourt, Brace & World, 1966.

Ure, Percy Neville. Justinian and His Age. Westport, Connecticut: Greenwood Press, 1979.

Vandercook, John W. *Empress of the Dusk*. New York: Reynal & Hitchcock, 1940. (Fictional account)

www.ingramcontent.com/pod-product-compliance
Lightning Source LLC
Chambersburg PA
CBHW072009090426
42734CB00033B/2325